The Markets for News

In the face of ongoing digitisation, *The Markets for News* examines how certain established economic features of the news industry have persisted and what makes them such stable frameworks for journalistic organisations.

Drawing on an analysis of Scandinavian news industries, this text revises journalism's economic foundations in the context of the algorithmically driven platform economy. Exploration of features such as journalism's two-sided market model, the network effect of platforms, and chain ownership, leads to a discussion about how journalism faces disruption from the introduction of artificial intelligence in the production, dissemination, and sale of news. As journalism undergoes transformations due to revenue losses, this book recognises a return to certain enduring features of journalism's organisational form, in particular the chain ownership form, that enables scale in adapting to platform logics and economics. This text serves as a basis for a theoretical discussion about strategic media management and critical political economy in the age of digital disruption.

This is an insightful book for academics and researchers in the fields of journalism, media industries, media policy, and communication studies.

Helle Sjøvaag is Professor of Journalism at the University of Stavanger, Norway. Her research focuses on the structural conditions for journalism, including its technology, economy, and regulation. She has published extensively on the digitalisation of the news industries, media pluralism and diversity, media systems, and journalistic professionalism.

Disruptions: Studies in Digital Journalism
Series editor: Bob Franklin

Disruptions refers to the radical changes provoked by the affordances of digital technologies that occur at a pace and on a scale that disrupts settled understandings and traditional ways of creating value, interacting and communicating both socially and professionally. The consequences for digital journalism involve far reaching changes to business models, professional practices, roles, ethics, products and even challenges to the accepted definitions and understandings of journalism. For Digital Journalism Studies, the field of academic inquiry which explores and examines digital journalism, disruption results in paradigmatic and tectonic shifts in scholarly concerns. It prompts reconsideration of research methods, theoretical analyses and responses (oppositional and consensual) to such changes, which have been described as being akin to 'a moment of mind-blowing uncertainty'.

Routledge's book series, *Disruptions: Studies in Digital Journalism*, seeks to capture, examine and analyse these moments of exciting and explosive professional and scholarly innovation which characterize developments in the day-to-day practice of journalism in an age of digital media, and which are articulated in the newly emerging academic discipline of Digital Journalism Studies.

Arab Digital Journalism
Noha Mellor

News Journalism and Twitter
Disruption, Adaption and Normalisation
Chrysi Dagoula

Digital Journalism and the Facilitation of Hate
Gregory P. Perreault

For more information about this series, please visit: www.routledge.com/Disruptions/book-series/DISRUPTDIGJOUR

The Markets for News

Enduring Structures in the Age of Business Model Disruptions

Helle Sjøvaag

LONDON AND NEW YORK

First published 2023
by Routledge
4 Park Square, Milton Park, Abingdon, Oxon OX14 4RN

and by Routledge
605 Third Avenue, New York, NY 10158

Routledge is an imprint of the Taylor & Francis Group, an informa business

British Library Cataloguing-in-Publication Data
A catalogue record for this book is available from the British Library

Library of Congress Cataloging-in-Publication Data
Names: Sjøvaag, Helle, author.
Title: The markets for news: enduring structures in the age of business model disruptions/Helle Sjøvaag.
Description: New York: Routledge, 2023. |
Series: Disruptions: studies in digital journalism | Includes bibliographical references and index. |
Identifiers: LCCN 2022031236 | ISBN 9780367533953 (hardback) | ISBN 9780367533960 (paperback) | ISBN 9781003081791 (ebook)
Subjects: LCSH: Newspaper publishing–Economic aspects–Scandinavia. | Newspaper publishing–Technological innovations.
Classification: LCC PN4734 .S55 2023 | DDC 078.5/722–dc23/eng/20220926
LC record available at https://lccn.loc.gov/2022031236

ISBN: 9780367533953 (hbk)
ISBN: 9780367533960 (pbk)
ISBN: 9781003081791 (ebk)

DOI: 10.4324/9781003081791

Typeset in Times New Roman
by Deanta Global Publishing Services, Chennai, India

Contents

Preface

Bob Franklin, the editor of this series, had asked me a few times if I would perhaps consider proposing a book on journalism's business models for this series on disruptions in digital journalism. Reluctant to take on this challenge, I thanked him for his confidence in me but declined because I did not feel suited to write about what money is to journalism in such a concrete manner. I am not an economist by training. I don't understand the maths of economics. And while I have written many articles and even a few books that place the market for news at the centre, it's not like any of that would be of value to an economist. My contributions are not to economic theory, they are to journalism theory.

One of those contributions is my first book in this series, *Journalism between the state and the market*, published in 2019. That book is an attempt to explain what the market is to journalism. What I argue in this book is that journalism is a business, and the business side of journalism should be considered part of the institution of journalism. After completing that book, I started noticing that other journalism scholars also had begun to mobilise the economic dimensions of journalism in their analyses, particularly in the context of technology change. I think it came from a necessity to understand how the economics of news works. Journalism's business model is broken, and we should understand why.

I had also become more drawn towards media industries studies. Not only did media industries researchers feel more eclectic in their choice of theory and method; I also felt that the efforts at theory development displayed signs of educational homophily within the journalism field. By that I mean that most journalism scholars come either from the profession or from sociology. My own educational background is the same. I was trained in the traditions and methods of sociology and the humanities, I have an undergraduate degree in journalism, and a master's degree in media studies. I started my university training in the late 1990s, when poststructuralism was a popular approach to media content and production. From then onwards, most of my professors have come from the critical tradition. I grew up reading Herman and Chomsky's propaganda model and Habermas' public sphere theory. Not once have I used these theories in my (published) work on journalism.

I started to move towards political economy and media economics during my PhD training. I had realised that if I was ever to get a job in academia, I would need to offer something complementary to the skills already present among the faculty. A risk, for sure, as hiring faculty tend to prefer like-minded individuals. But I knew the critical perspective would be well covered in the future. So I decided to diversify my theoretical competences. I began reading media economics textbooks and research articles. The concreteness of that literature appealed to me. Here were some actual tools to understand what was going on with journalism, not just critical reflections on what was wrong with journalism. From then on, most of my research has been industry or economy 'adjacent'. I tend to be agnostic and pragmatic about how journalism works as a profession and as an industry. I care more about why things are the way they are than how things should be. Escaping my critical political economy training was easy, actually, but reviewers have always made sure that my work stays within the appropriate boundaries of the critical tradition. This is of course due to the journals I have published in and their reviewer pool. I have never published in an economics journal.

But then I thought, so what if I don't have an economics background? Perhaps it's even a good idea to write a book about the markets for news from the perspective of a journalism scholar. Most reference work on market perspectives are written by media economists and media management researchers. And while I do not pretend to rival them in any respect, this is at least a chance to apply the issues in media economics that are relevant to journalism – to essentially skip over many of the aspects that are more cultural industries oriented. This has been a real challenge in many respects, not least because many of the economic principles and theories applied to journalism are facing obsolescence at this point. I have had little to go on here, in rethinking how differentiation, two-sided markets, free-riding, and market failure apply to journalism in the platform economy. To that end, this book must be said to be exploratory.

Moreover, finding a way to reconcile the different theoretical perspectives on journalism as an industry has been an uncomfortable exercise at times. While the aim was really to juxtapose media management theory with critical political economy to arrive at a framework for looking at journalism's business model in the digital economy, concluding one way or another about the two frameworks was not easy. Instead, I ended up where I always end up – with a more institutionally oriented perspective on what markets mean to journalism as a profession. While I ended up in a familiar place, I did discover new ways to look at economic behaviour from the theories of the new economic sociology – an entirely novel perspective, for me at least, that helped me to understand better some of mechanisms I have observed about news markets over the years. In fact it solved much of the discomfort I have for the normativity of the critical political economy perspective as well as tempered some of the urgency for action often felt within the management field. As my aim is neither to blame nor to fix journalism, this is a good place to be for me.

My thanks, therefore, to Bob Franklin, for the opportunity to write about markets for an audience of journalism researchers. I also wish to thank the Ander Foundation and the Research Council of Norway for providing the funding to do the research required for this book. Thanks also to my project collaborators and co-authors, without which this book would not be possible. They are listed in the introductory chapter. And finally, a very special thanks to Aske Kammer, Raul Ferrer-Conill, and Nina Kvalheim for valuable conversations along the way and not least for concrete feedback in preparing the draft for this book.

Stavanger, May 2022

1 Two waves of digital disruption

This is a book about how journalism makes money. This is a fundamental issue because the business side of journalism is as much a part of the institution as the editorial side. How news media make money, why they lose money, or whether or not they need to make a profit at all, impacts on their journalism. Where news makes a profit also matters. The question here is what kind of market the news market is, and in what kinds of markets news can make money. This question is all the more pressing because the markets for news have changed dramatically.

When Iris Chyi and Ori Tenenboim (2019a) looked at where revenue came from in American local newspapers, they found that the bulk of the income still derives from the printed edition. They also found that readers tend to value the print product more than the online product. This led them to ask an important question (Chyi & Tenenboim, 2019b): why do local newspapers need to go digital at all, when their main value lies with print, and the push towards digital only serves to deplete the quality of their most valued asset? To provide one possible answer to that question, we can look at cost and revenue streams. How do news media spend money, and how do they make money?

Traditionally, journalism's income has been based in audience and advertising revenue. Most media in the world are commercial entities (Noam, 2018), meaning they are for-profit organisations with owners, investors, or shareholders whose motivations are at least partly (if not mostly) based on making money from their investment. Commercial media have operated in two-sided markets. They draw revenue from direct sales or subscriptions to customers who buy the editorial product, and they generate income from businesses that seek the attention of these customers through purchasing advertising space. As two-sided markets have network effects (Rochet & Tirole, 2006), the value of one side is dependent on the other. The more users there are in the network, the higher the value of the network. The classic example of such network effects is the telephone – useless as long as there is only one user, but invaluable when everyone is connected.

DOI: 10.4324/9781003081791-1

For the newspaper, the number and type of subscribers it has determines its value to advertisers. If a newspaper reaches elite audiences, it will typically attract advertising from producers of high-end products. If a newspaper can boast the largest readership in the market, it has more power in setting prices. When advertising space is not a scarce resource, but rather in competition with more elite, quality, or larger media, newspapers have less power in setting prices. This is known as the umbrella model of newspaper markets (Lacy, 1991; Rosse, 1975). Based on advertising market mechanisms, it describes how ad markets are segmented according to horizontal or vertical competition. Small, local newspapers in these markets cannot afford to compete with larger metropolitan newspapers operating in their area, hence they lower their prices to attract advertisers who cannot afford to buy ad space in the metropolitan edition. Traditionally, this has meant that local trade and commerce tend to advertise in local media, while retail chains tend to prefer, and can afford, wider-reaching and more generalist outlets.

Over the past decades, however, local retail has become chainified, narrowing the ad markets in local news segments. Moreover, retail now tends to funnel its ad campaigns through advertising agencies. As these agencies tend to prefer coordinated campaigns, newspaper chains have grown more attractive than independent papers, causing a concentration in ownership. It is easier for local newspapers to bring in advertising revenue if they are part of a larger chain than if they stand on their own. Hence, smaller publishers have begun to seek corporate ownership. The mechanisms of the advertising market thus have a structural effect on journalism, incentivising increased concentration. Since 2014, the umbrella market model has been further disrupted by the advent of programmatic advertising, where artificial intelligence is used to automatically link advertising messages with users, based on user metrics generated by media companies to meet the competition from Google and Facebook. Advertising is driven by data rather than reach, changing the ways in which news media need to tailor their environments to remain relevant to advertisers.

So, the reason why local newspapers do not just focus on the print edition is that the advertising market has shifted to the point where print advertising generates less and less income. Even local, independent retailers and businesses prefer Google and Facebook over their local paper. Google and Facebook can reach potential customers locally because they have masses of behavioural and purchasing data on users everywhere. Not only do local newspapers no longer reach a cross-section of local readers – their subscribers tend to be seniors rather than millennials – they also lack the analytics to compete with Google and Facebook. Without a strong online presence, and without the volume of output and users needed to perform reliable analytics, local papers are getting disconnected from advertising revenue. Both scale and skills are important if local news want to latch onto the market for programmatic advertising. Moreover, off-the-shelf solutions are no longer sufficient to perform sophisticated analytics. As a result, digital costs rise – both in terms of software and in terms of manpower. To offset these costs, local papers need to merge with larger organisational entities. Not only does this allow them to piggyback on corporate digital marketing tools, the volume of data that a chain operation can have on content and readers also solves the problem of scale in the same go. Hence, the shift towards AI technology presents an entirely different set of market mechanisms that journalism must relate to. AI enables platforms to expand their networks. The value here is not products, but users. To link users and suppliers in these networks, platforms need data to enable valuable interactions. To participate in this economy, news media need to ready their data for platform complementarity.

Adjusting to developments in technology has been a problem for journalism since the launch of the internet. However, before the introduction of AI in the form of programmatic advertising and audience analytics, local newspapers had several advantages that deterred digital innovations in local news structures. For one thing, the winner-takes-all nature of online advertising meant there was no point in local papers moving online. Doomed to fail in the competition with the upper layers of the umbrella structure, local papers reserved their unique and locally valuable content for the print edition. In systems with press support such as in Scandinavia, state support was also largely tied to print circulation, which further deterred online production. Analogue-inclined older readers also preferred the print edition; and going digital too fast could mean scaring loyal customers away. In addition, the cost of having an online edition depleted the resources for print, causing potential deterioration of the highly valued print product. Once digital publishing solutions also needed more customisation, costs rose further. The advertising side of the local publishing operation continued to rely on person-to-person interaction through direct sales, losing valuable innovation experience in the process. The slow adaptation to online publishing that many local newspapers embraced in the digital transition has thus left them poorly situated in a second transition – the transition to AI.

Waves of disruption

The digitalisation of the news industries has been on the research agenda in journalism studies since the introduction of the internet. It is important to note, however, that we are not talking about just one, continuous, digital transformation here. Scholarship sometimes seems to treat digitalisation as a single process. I would rather argue that journalism has undergone two digital transformations. First, journalism adjusted to the potential for interaction, with audience engagement, user generated content, and facilitating feedback and discussion. These adjustments took place in the early 2000s. Since the mid-2010s, journalism has entered the data-driven platform economy, faced with AI-driven processes including audience analytics, personalisation, and programmatic advertising operating in a global, multi-sided marketplace. This track change mobilises new economic principles. The core business model of platforms is the extraction, analysis, and monetisation of data (Hintz et al., 2018). Journalism is just one content among many that these algorithmic processes match with users. Moreover, platforms are agnostic about content, to the extent that product quality is less relevant. Hence, not only has the market in which the journalistic product competes expanded; the basis for competitive advantage has shifted. To support this supposition, I will briefly summarise how the economic and industry-related issues raised by scholarship reflect these two phases. I will then demonstrate how and when this shift occurred by using the Reuters Institute Digital News Report as an empirical case in mapping the digital transformations of the news industries.

While industry perspectives on digital journalism are present in the research only to a limited extent (Steensen & Ahva, 2015), early transformation studies were often contextualised in economic discourse, particularly as to how journalism will be financed in the digital age (Steensen et al., 2019). Questions about this transformation were often framed within a crisis narrative (Brüggemann et al., 2016; Mensing & Ryfe, 2013), and largely revolved around revenues (Mensing, 2007) and business models (Kaye & Quinn, 2010). Scholars launched a number of solutions to this crisis, suggesting journalistic organisations turn towards concepts like entrepreneurialism (Baines & Kennedy, 2010; Gynnild, 2014), startup thinking (Briggs, 2012; Chadha, 2016), and media labs (Capoano & Ranieri, 2016), often relying on niche theory (e.g., Cook & Sirkunen, 2013; Walck et al., 2015). Studies also probed different approaches to online revenues, including differentiation, versionality, and substitution (van der Wurff, 2011); readership and willingness-to-pay (Goyanes, 2014); paid content (Brandstetter & Schmalhofer, 2014) and advertising (Picard, 2008). Most of these studies were motivated by the news industries' loss of income in the audience and advertising markets. Early disruption studies thus typically had an organisational focus, looking at the introduction of new technology, convergence processes, and new modes of production (Berte & De Bens, 2009).

Studies looking at the second wave of digitalisation of the news industries – the turn to AI – have focused more on ecosystem adaptation

(Anderson et al., 2015), including cost adjustment to withstand income losses (Evens, 2018), and organisational restructuring to merge journalism and tech cultures (Küng, 2017). Efforts are also made to adapt the product and production to this new reality, including content adjustments such as the personalisation of content (Kunert & Thurman, 2019), optimisation of content management (Chan-Olmsted, 2019), and robotisation of journalistic production (Bucher, 2018). The term most often used to describe this shift is 'post-industrialisation' (Deuze & Witschge, 2018). Here, news media find they need to expand the network externalities of their operations to include third-party intermediaries (Cawley, 2019) and social media platforms (van Dijck et al., 2018). There is more focus on partnerships (Sjøvaag & Owren, 2021a) and diversification of business models (Jenkins & Nielsen, 2018), as the news industries struggle to retain their value to customers in both markets. To that end, the narrative in both these phases is about adaptability and adjustment. As digital intermediaries, social media, and platforms move in to shape the media ecology, editorial organisations have tried their best to reap the benefits of these changes, looking for opportunities to survive as their markets change.

A look into the Reuters Institute Digital News Report reveals the speed and impact of this development. Published annually since 2012, the Report outlines the major technological developments from year to year, revealing the ways in which the programmatic shift has impacted on journalism. In 2012 (Newman, 2012), the focus was still on the switch from print to digital. News organisations were declaring digital first strategies, even though there was low willingness-to-pay for online news. Smartphone news consumption was becoming an issue, and search and social media were already important channels for news consumption. A keyword from the 2012 edition is 'monetisation' – the search for digital income. Another is 'multi-platform', the utilisation of multiple channels to reach audiences. Hence, while news media found new ways to get their products out to readers, they struggled to make this increased reach profitable.

In 2013 (Newman & Levy, 2013), search engines and social media are described as the 'new gatekeepers' of news. Mobile and social news consumption is on the rise. Business model disruption is a key concern, solutions to which are identified as 'niche orientation' and 'paywalls'. The digital shift is seen as imperative, but the report also notes that it is important to keep in mind the loyal print buyers. Paywall presents a way to identify and retain these loyal customers, while niche orientation presents avenues for competitive advantage through co-existence. In 2014, the speed of this transformation comes to fruition, described as "a new wave of disruption" (Newman & Levy, 2014, p. 8). This is not least because mobile use and social media news consumption increase rapidly.

The impact of this shift also becomes apparent across sectors. The report now grows more detailed in its mapping of technological change. It also widens the scope of media use situations, portals, and devices that are mapped in news consumption, signalling the extent to which the news ecology is expanding.

The 2015 report (Newman et al., 2015) illustrates the speed of change particularly well. New realities include news aggregation and online video, smartwatches, native advertising, mobile alerts, and native-born players, noting also rising fears over filter bubbles. The smartphone is described as the defining device for news, disruptive to the industry. Search engines and social media grow more important as gateways to the news, and the transparency of Facebook's algorithms becomes an issue. Platforms and digital intermediaries enter the frame in 2016 (Newman et al., 2016), as do questions around personalised news and algorithmic news curation. Social media for news takes over, Facebook being the dominant gatekeeper. In this context, Facebook's 'instant articles' feature is portrayed as a major problem for journalism's business model. Snapchat is also growing fast at this point, and live social video is on the rise. News companies begin to cut staff, as they find it hard to monetise online readers. Paywall strategies are being rolled back, and news outlets begin to try out new income sources such as membership models. As branded content grows, news organisations launch internal brand studios of their own. There is increasing influence from platforms and algorithms, the report noting that it 'feels like the beginning of a new phase of media disruption' (p. 28). The years 2015–2016 thus represent a major change, with both years described as disruptive to the news industries, in particular caused by shifting gateways and the introduction of algorithmic news curation.

In 2017 (Newman et al., 2017), social media news use flattens out, while messaging apps like WhatsApp are on the rise. There is a Trump effect on U.S. subscription trends, and regulators get involved over concerns of the effects of Google and Facebook's algorithms. Trust issues also rise as a result of fake news and viral algorithms. Voice activated digital assistants like Alexa enter the market, and mobile begins to take over home media use. The growth in push notifications leads to a comeback for news apps, but there is little improvement in display advertising for the mobile screen, lowering monetisation potentials. The report also notes the effects of Facebook's algorithm change in 2016 that prioritised friends over news, causing a downturn in social media revenue for news companies. Automation begins to take effect, as news organisations innovate their paywall models by using big data models to predict churn and dynamic differential pricing. As for monetisation, there is a rise in non-profits. We also see the first mention of 'news avoidance'.

In 2018 (Newman et al., 2018), donations emerge as a monetisation strategy, podcasts make a comeback, and the growth in social media for news comes to a halt, caused in large part by Facebook's algorithm change towards 'meaningful interactions'. Another comeback in 2018 is the email alert, used to bring readers to the site directly, surpassing intermediaries. Subscription takes an upturn, and there is an industry-wide focus on reader payments, as the online advertising model goes into decline. Data privacy and misinformation are major concerns, and this year also sees an increase in alternative and partisan media.

Platform power comes to full fruition in 2019 (Newman et al., 2019). This is, however, a difficult year for social media, particularly for Facebook and YouTube, as concerns over privacy and misinformation grow. Facebook Watch shifts video towards longer formats, making short news more difficult to monetise. This, as well as other recent changes, ultimately makes Facebook appear less and less friendly to news consumption. Instead, mobile news aggregation grows. Bundles of multiple brands emerge to ease users' access and payment in an effort to offset continued revenue losses and staff cuts. In 2020 (Newman et al., 2020) there is a significant increase in payment for news, in large part due to the coronavirus pandemic. News becomes even more distributed, with weaker connections to websites and apps. Instead, news use shifts more towards private messaging like WhatsApp and social media like Instagram. Advertising revenue continues to decline, while paywalls tighten. Among payment models online we now find subscriptions, donations, memberships, and micropayments. At the same time, misinformation remains a concern, and there is a rise in distrust in mainstream news.

The 2021 report (Newman et al., 2021) shows that trusted brands do well through the coronavirus lockdown, and there is a rise in trust in news in general. At the same time, messaging apps like WhatsApp and Telegram fuel concerns over the spread of misinformation. The pandemic also speeds up the death of print, accelerating the digital shift as distribution is halted during lockdown. The retraction of advertising spending during the pandemic also leads to further lay-offs in the news industries. Online news payment remains low except for in certain wealthy countries like the Nordics, but subscription and membership models accelerate. News avoidance is still an issue, and the smartphone for news use continues to grow in importance. For traditional news markets, winner-takes-all effects are demonstrated, but multiple subscriptions are becoming more common in mature markets. Nevertheless, local newspapers are heavily affected by internet platforms, and blind spots are developing in most markets, noting a rise in concern for the future of local media among regulators as well as industry.

As this annual rundown of the Reuters Institute Digital News Report demonstrates, news organisations continue to search for new revenue streams as platforms and algorithms make disruptive introductions to the news industries mid-decade. Notably, this 'new phase of media disruption' occurs in 2016, when platforms begin to dominate the field. As news consumption shifts from online to mobile, news companies struggle to reach audiences as a brand in their own right, relying in large part on intermediary platforms to circulate news. Trends are not, however, the same across all countries surveyed. The 2018 and 2019 editions both contain optimistic notes about news in the Nordic countries. Nordic news media seem to have a stronger relationship with their readers, shown in their tendency to prefer the app or website of their news provider over so-called side-doors. The 2021 report also shows that Norwegian audiences have more attachment to their local newspaper. The authors link this Nordic divergence from the general trends to higher willingness-to-pay for news in the region. Brand power can thus be seen to enable user payment even in markets with a strong third-party platform presence.

The news markets in the Nordics are thus a particular case in point, worthy of closer examination. Nordic audiences have higher news use, higher trust in institutions, higher satisfaction with their public service broadcasters, and higher willingness-to-pay for news. While Nordic news organisations are often described as leaders in business model innovation (Barland, 2013), their models are also firmly based in established organisational arrangements – journalism's enduring features. They still rely on the two-sided market model with income from users and advertisers. Moreover, the model of chain ownership persists. In this book, I will take a closer look at what characterises these enduring forms of journalistic organisation, asking to what extent they are disrupted by the power of platforms and algorithms.

Research design

The book is based on research conducted within two research projects: *Digital News Agendas in Scandinavia* (2018–2022), funded by the Ander Foundation in Sweden; and *The Datafication of Communicative Power: Towards an Independent Media Policy for Norway's Digital Infrastructures* (2021–2025), funded by the Research Council of Norway. With these projects, I have sought to understand the impact of digitalisation on Scandinavian news industries, focusing on the networked structure of news, the role of platforms in the digital news ecology, processes of ownership consolidation in the newspaper markets, and risk management in news industries. With a clear industry orientation, the aim of these projects has been to establish the big-picture impact of platforms and infrastructures on journalism and its business models, and consolidation processes at the ownership level. Analyses are based on a mix of quantitative and qualitative data, including about 80 million hyperlink connections (Sjøvaag, et al., 2019) and roughly one million social media posts from around 500 news outlets in Denmark, Norway, and Sweden (Ferrer-Conill et al., 2021; Haim et al., 2021); in-depth semi-structured interviews with eight editors-in-chief undergoing consolidation in Norway (Sjøvaag et al., 2021), and five newspaper CEOs in Denmark, Norway, and Sweden (Sjøvaag & Owren, 2021a, b); as well as infrastructure mappings of the digital media landscape in Norway. Methods employed include hyperlink network analysis, automated text analysis, semi-structured interviews, and thematic analysis. The scholars involved in the project include professor Michael Karlsson from Karlstad University, associate professor Aske Kammer at Roskilde University, associate professor Raul Ferrer Conill from the University of Stavanger, professor Mario Haim from Ludwig-Maximilians University of Munich, professor Wouter van Atteveld from Frei University Amsterdam, professor Dag Elgesem from the University of Bergen, as well as postdoc candidate Nina Kvalheim and PhD candidate Thomas Owren from the University of Stavanger. The projects have been based at the University of Stavanger, Norway.

What I present in this book is an approach to thinking about the markets for news given the structural changes impacting journalism as an institution in the Nordic region. During the course of working on these projects, two realities have become apparent in particular. The first is empirical in nature, the other theoretical. The empirical reality is that while things are changing fast, much still remains the same. There has been a lot of talk of innovation in the Nordic news industries, but the Scandinavian news organisations have mainly been able to survive by focusing on core values in journalism. The agile shift towards AI application in news curation and audience analytics that many companies have managed is due in large part to established professionalism, ownership cultures, and a differentiated press system based on pluralist welfare state principles (cf. Syvertsen et al., 2014), including, in particular, systems of state support that enjoy strong cross-party consensus and industry support. As independent local newspapers move to chain ownership, media systems properties matter for how pluralism is retained in the system (cf. Sjøvaag, 2019).

The theoretical insight I have gained from working on these issues is that the field of journalism is struggling to grasp the economic effects of digitalisation on the news industries in large part because of the legacy of critical political economy. Averse to tackling the issues of income, business models, ownership, and advertising ourselves, journalism scholars tend to shy away from media management perspectives, relying more on the familiar writings of critical political economy scholars embedded in us since our student days. There is a fundamental conflict between the two perspectives. Media management tends to see innovation as the solution to everything. Critical political economy tends to see profit (and thus ownership) as the cause of everything. Media management and economics thus sees solutions in the organisation and the markets, while critical political economy only sees solutions within the system of state support. Engaging with the business side of journalism, and in particular in talking with newspaper CEOs, it has become clear to me that news managers' understanding lies somewhere in between. While they largely speak with the language of management studies, their motivations are fully embedded in the professional ethos and the media system properties in which they operate. They are critical of the market while also seeking solutions in the market. So why is it that we as scholars struggle so much to bridge this divide?

The resistance to such an 'agnostic' approach has become most evident to me during the processes of peer review. Reviewers simply refuse to take managers' statements at face value, evidence of the suspicion that critical political economy has left us with regarding those who seek, or work to increase, profit. Such 'field policing' leaves little room for bridging theoretical divides. Nor does it help in critically reflecting on the hegemony of critical political economy within media studies. While we should always be critical of grand-standing statements made when sources of power speak to researchers, we seldom extend the same suspicion to the journalists or editors we interview. Regardless of how 'strategic' CEO speech may be, they still speak within a logic of appropriateness (Fligstein, 2015) that considers the reality as well as the ideal. To understand the news industries, then, we need to understand the framework that shapes news managers' perceptions and decision-making. That includes not only Silicon Valley-inspired rhetoric; it also reflects the norms of the institution – an institution that is inherently critical to power.

This book is my process to find a way to exist within these paradigms, and hopefully, to find ways in which they can inform and strengthen each other. To that end, the outline of this book follows an exploratory design. The first thing to do is to get a firm grasp of the nuts and bolts of how journalism makes money. Once we have a clear image of journalism's business model and how it is challenged by the shift to AI, we move on to examine news markets empirically, by looking at consolidation trends in the Scandinavian newspaper markets in light of market failure. Next, we examine how revenue is understood within the two theoretical directions of critical political economy and media management and economics. We then go on to set these developments within the framework of platform economics and how the shift to AI affects news media's business models. We end up, finally, with an assessment of the two dominant frameworks of critical political economy and media management, the aim of which is to interrogate fundamental assumptions in journalism studies about the place of profit in the institution of journalism.

Introducing the chapters

This introduction has outlined the problems facing news organisations in the shift to programmatic advertising and audience analytics that presents news organisations with costs they are unable to sustain alone. Chyi and Tenenboim's argument (2019b) addressing the question of the print/digital futures of local newspapers in the U.S. has been mobilised to outline two distinct phases of digitalisation, the first being about getting online, the second being about the shift to AI. The ten previous editions of the Reuters Institute Digital News Report have been analysed to illustrate this shift and the extent of impact brought on by platforms and AI technology.

Chapter 2 will look more closely into the stable and presumed enduring forms of journalism's organisation. I explain the basic concepts of journalism's two-sided market and outline the characteristics of news markets. Here, I explore the extent to which core economic principles of media markets still hold true, including the notion that news is a public good, to what extent differentiation still works as a strategy, and how non-substitutable news really is. I then go on to explain the cost structure of news, the aim of which is to illustrate the mechanisms for making money within the news industries in the traditional market model for news. Next, I explore how journalism's two-sided business model is challenged by the switch to AI technology, and consider what advertising means to journalism's revenue model in the two phases of digitalisation. Finally, I examine what organisational and financial features of journalism remain relevant, and how core assumptions about news as a product are challenged by the platform economy.

As Chapter 1 outlines, the effects of revenue generation on both sides of the market in the context of digital disruption led to a concentration of ownership to attain scale advantages. Chapter 3 discusses the contentious issue of concentration and its relationship to the concept of market failure. I use consolidation in the Scandinavian newspaper markets as an example of how digital disruption affects independent ownership, local dispersed newspaper structures, ownership forms, consolidation, and its impact on the two sides of the market. Relevant in this discussion is the return to enduring organisational forms of chain ownership, and how the expansion of the media ecology alters the perceptions surrounding mergers and acquisitions in the Scandinavian news industries.

The fourth chapter sets out to interrogate the two main theoretical perspectives mobilised to analyse the business of journalism: strategic management perspectives and critical political economy. They are juxtaposed in particular in the way revenue and ownership are conceptualised in how they impact on journalism. To that end, the chapter seeks to engage in a discussion of the merits of the two perspectives in the context of market disruption. At the end of this chapter, I offer a third perspective in the form of economic sociology, the aim of which is to link familiar aspects of institutionalism in journalism research to theoretical perspectives on the news media as an industry.

In Chapter 5 I return to the issue of market changes by examining what is different about platform economics and how it challenges journalism's business model. By considering how journalism has responded to these new economic realities, I also use this discussion to examine the explanatory power of the two theoretical frameworks outlined in the previous chapter. The alternative framework of institutional economics is mobilised to examine how journalism's response to the shift towards an AI-driven economy can be explained by the enduring features in journalism's institutional organisation.

The final chapter provides a short summary of the arguments presented in the book, linking theoretical perspectives to journalism's two stages of digitalisation, elevating disruption to an ongoing process whose shifting conditions require theoretical flexibility and ongoing revision. The concluding chapter seeks to engage in a discussion about the enduring forms of journalism and their impact on news production. Enduring forms in this context not only focus on journalism's organisation such as the two-sided market model or chain ownership, but also refer to news media's path dependent regulatory frameworks, their media systems' contexts, and the theoretical frameworks used to understand journalism's transformations. More than anything, the conclusion argues that journalism research needs to consider more broadly how news media's business and industry features shape the profession and its various expressions. Returning to Chyi and Tenenboim's questions about journalism's digital futures, the final chapter also seeks to look beyond the Scandinavian context.

2 The enduring forms of journalism's organisation

This chapter outlines the main characteristics of news products. Many of the long-standing concepts used to describe journalism as a commodity, such as two-sided markets, differentiation, and substitution, have become challenged or even obsolete as descriptors of news markets in an AI-driven context. In this chapter, I try to sort through these concepts as they apply to the platform ecology and the algorithmically curated news ecosystem. The aim here is to provide an overview of terms used to describe and analyse news markets while also taking stock of their usefulness or applicability today, thus performing an evaluation of the vocabulary used and the impact of AI on the theory of journalism's markets. Despite the game-changing properties of AI on journalism, few studies acknowledge the extent to which this alters the fundamental principles of the news industries. Whereas the news value chain is based in supply-side economics (Van Alstyne et al., 2016), where value accumulates through the chain from resource through production to assembly and distribution, the platform economy on which news organisations have come to rely is based in demand-side economics, where supply and demand meet through the platform itself. The positive network effects that the news industries once held as a platform connecting users and advertisers has now shifted to search and social media giants Google, Facebook, and YouTube. As news organisations struggle to retain income in this competitive space, journalism's network effects move to a higher structural level – through chain formations securing monopolies in regional markets. The chapter thus links the two-sided business model with the newspaper chain as a particular form of organising journalistic labour.

The characteristics of news markets

Media markets are different from normal commodities markets because media are also public goods. Media products are non-excludable. They are not 'used up' by one person's consumption the way other products are, like

DOI: 10.4324/9781003081791-2

toothpaste or apples. Hence, media products are non-excludable and non-depletable public goods where one individual's consumption does not interfere with its availability to another (Chan-Olmsted, 2006). Moreover, one person's use does not detract from the value of the product to another user (Garnham, 2014; Hamilton, 2004). Two people can read the same newspaper without it affecting the product. Particularly in the online realm, news products can be easily circulated after they are published (Ryfe, 2021). Media products are therefore non-rivalrous. One person's use does not exclude others from using it.

Media goods are also experience goods. This means you have to experience them in order to judge the quality of the product (Hamilton, 2004, p. 9). It is difficult to know beforehand whether a newspaper article, a song or a movie is to your taste without experiencing it. This means there is no inherent scarcity of media products (Garnham, 2014). In most news markets, and particularly in digital markets, there is an over-supply of news. What is scarce in this context is attention, not content (Evens, 2018). Moreover, media products carry positive externalities. They have value beyond their own use. Whether or not you follow the news yourself, it still presents a value to society that people are generally informed about what goes on in the world. Public goods are goods that benefit society beyond the economic transaction itself. Journalism is therefore a merit good – goods that society needs, but that individuals typically undervalue, and thus the market tends to under produce (Ali, 2016; Olsen et al., 2020). Merit good markets tend to be regulated to preserve the public interest (Picard, 2017). This is why public libraries and museums are publicly funded, and why certain media receive state support, such as public service broadcasters (cf. Allern & Pollack, 2019).

These basic assumptions about the market characteristics of news have been challenged by developments in news use over recent years. Scholars have recently debated the public and merit good status of journalism, both in the U.S. context (Napoli, 2020; Pickard, 2019; Walters, 2020), and in Europe (Murschetz, 2020), often pointing to journalism's problem in sustaining these virtues in the face of economic and technological changes. As Peters (2019) remarks, not everyone has access to journalism, and not everyone is interested in journalism. Digital paywalls, coupled with the defunding of public service broadcasting (Sjøvaag & Ohlsson, 2019) detract from the universal access needed for a product to be a merit good (cf. Usher, 2021). Moreover, says Peters (2019), populism, echo chambers and compassion fatigue challenge the spirit of the positive externalities and non-rivalrous nature of journalism. While news is still a non-excludable experience good, journalism's ability to provide value to society is challenged by increased polarisation, a decline of mainstream news in many parts of the world, the effects of social media, and rising costs in accessing news.

Nevertheless, the public good characteristics of media products make it difficult to exclude free-riding. People can rather easily enjoy media goods without paying for them, e.g., by reading their roommate's magazine or newspaper, or borrowing their movies or CDs. The digitalisation of media products and the personalisation of media use through the mobile phone, however, means that free-riding is not as easy as it used to be. It is more cumbersome to access another person's music library or streaming service than to borrow a physical copy. Subscription paywalls, login features, and algorithmic curation, not to mention app use, have largely personalised media use. Free-riding is thus necessarily a largely voluntary practice – friends sharing their friends' streaming accounts. As free-riding amounts to an overuse of public goods without paying for them, it often leads to inferior products (Fengler & Ruß-Mohl, 2008). Low sales figures tend to keep companies from investing in products that few want to pay for. Not least because the cost of preventing free-riding is usually higher than the value companies can get from adding a single customer (Garnham, 2014). The free-riding problem is another reason why public goods are often subsidised by government funding.

One could consider search engines' use of news snippets in their display of search results as free-riding (Scalzini, 2021). Google arguably capitalises on investments made in the news industries (Colangelo, 2022) to satisfy the search needs of their users, to the extent that it threatens the business model of the creative industries (Humphreys & Simpson, 2018). The extended meaning of free-riding thus explains how one firm benefits from the efforts of another without paying the cost (Kathuria & Lai, 2020). Too much free-riding by third parties such as Google lowers incentives for news organisations to make proper investments, and can lead to the underproduction of quality news. In this situation, market failure is a threat. Market failure occurs when the market is no longer able to effectively allocate important goods and services (Pickard, 2017). When businesses can no longer extract the returns needed to justify their spending, for instance if customers stop paying for the product, market failure can occur. Here we enter the domain of copyright law and intellectual property rights. News media have found it difficult to enforce copyright on news because they ultimately need to circulate information (Slauter, 2019). Hence, while user free-riding has been made less easy by the shift to handheld devices, firm free-riding has been made easier. Facebook and Google are able to capitalise on investments in journalism made in the news industries in the form of advertising income.

Regardless of the free-riding problem in the mobile AI-driven transformation, news products still have public goods characteristics with potential positive externalities. The problem for journalism is that the markets have changed. Normal markets constitute exchanges of goods and services where the producers seek to satisfy consumer taste (Meehan & Torre, 2014; Peterson & Anand, 2004). Whereas media markets could be rather diverse markets, as consumers have a wide variety of tastes, the concept of 'popular taste' means that there is potential for a mass market. In order to maximise consumer share, producers are incentivised to pursue popular tastes over marginal tastes, leading to a homogenisation of media products. With limited competition, producers will seek to satisfy maximum, mean consumer preference, preferring competition over a costly differentiation strategy (Hollifield, 2006).

This is referred to as Hotelling's law. Harold Hotelling demonstrated in 1929 how firms producing similar products tend to move towards the largest consumer groups. This explains why coffee shops tend to locate on the same street. Hotelling observed that the most profitable location is right next to a competitor in the middle of the geographic or product market. He used ice cream sellers at a beach as example. Given this duopoly situation (two vendors serving the entire market), the ice cream sellers would position themselves at the entry of the beach. They would both prefer to compete to reach a potential majority of customers than divide the beach between them to secure only half the market. Moreover, their products would be highly similar, displaying a substitute offer of ice cream choices. If ice cream stand number one has popular products, leading to long queues, ice cream stand number two will provide similar products, offering substitutes and distributing customers. This law has been demonstrated also in media markets, where audience preferences tend to concentrate in the middle of the market, resulting in an excess of similar offers in the centre, for instance in duopoly television markets (Anderson et al., 2010).

The concept of a mass market is, however, currently being disrupted by audience analytics and AI enabling user targeting and personalisation. Former Wired editor Chris Anderson (2004, 2006) once described the online market as a "long tail". Here, content abundance suggests that diversified tastes, as well as an abundance of access points, would make it more difficult to attain blockbuster hits. The long tail thesis thus explains how the media industries would be increasingly oriented towards niche markets with relatively small demand (Hesmondhalgh, 2013). Anderson posited that the online market could satisfy a potentially endless demand for diversified products. An online bookstore like Amazon can stock millions of specialised publications that a physical bookstore cannot possibly hold. In a global market space, the income potential also becomes greater for specialised products, as potential customers are not limited to the physical sales area. To that end, while markets may still be "determined by products consumers will substitute for each other" (Lacy & Noh, 1997, p. 8), they are not so much defined by geography.

Anderson argued that long-tail markets only have room for a few big blockbusters with massive revenue potential. What AI has demonstrated, however, is how data analytics can be used to gain insight into audience tastes, which in turn can be used to *design* hits, or at least increase the possibility that a production will become a hit. The famous example here is how Netflix used popularity data to attract users to its streaming service by releasing *House of Cards*, a creative decision that was based on combining the most popular show (the original U.K. production of *House of Cards*), with the then most popular actor (Kevin Spacey) (Evens, 2018). This is arguably also what newspapers do when they use audience data to find out what kind of stories readers prefer, what kind of stories they share on social media, and what kind of stories convert browsers to paying customers. The potential downside to this effect for merit goods is that media companies prioritise proven formulas over product innovation. Moreover, news organisations often feel intermediaries give them insufficient or incomplete data, which makes it difficult to assess performance and establish benchmarks to evaluate success (Kleis Nielsen & Ganter, 2018).

Producers aim for mass markets because differentiating products is costly. When mass market strategies are successful, they can become winner-takes-all markets – markets where one producer earns a lot more than the other competitors. News markets can easily become winner-takes-all markets, especially in two-sided markets where advertisers prefer to place their ads with the largest channel rather than dealing with multiple outlets. Two-sided markets are markets where a firm produces two different commodities that can be sold to separate and distinct user groups (Doyle, 2013). For journalism, this amounts on the one side to audiences that buy the news product, and on the other, to the advertisers that seek these news reading audiences. In effect, newspapers are 'sold twice' – first to readers who buy the content and second to advertisers (Gabszewicz et al., 2002).

This feature is what helped incumbents to capture the advertising market when newspapers went online in the 1990s. Large news organisations were replete with resources to build websites that attracted users to their free news services, thereby also attracting advertisers (Sjøvaag et al., 2019). Advertisers would favour one top site over multiple smaller ones to maximise exposure and save costs. In this economy, it was difficult for smaller sites to attract enough online advertising revenue to offset losses on the print side of the market. Hence, the two-sided market was still in effect for a decade or so, with heavy winner-takes-all characteristics, from when newspapers went online in the mid-1990s until search and social media began to attract advertising, Google in 2000 and Facebook in 2007. The winner-takes-all effects of the two-sided news market have not lost their power with the move to AI. While advertisers are only concerned with reaching the right audience, attracting that potential audience is still important. Incumbent market leaders have an advantage also in this market, as they have the scale of data to satisfy the analytics needs of advertisers. Media product markets are therefore still two-sided markets, linking audiences with advertisers, but they are no longer the only platform connecting the two. To that end, digital news markets have been described as multi-sided markets, with media operating as multi-sided platforms relying on multiple interaction channels and serving multiple categories of agents (Gabszewicz et al., 2015).

Platforms, in the sense of the extended media ecology, are gatekeepers that control the flow of information. Platforms hold strategically important market positions because they offer common functionalities and complementarity between products. Platforms thus have natural network effects (Ballon & Van Heesvelde, 2011). Network effects describe how the value of network systems increases with each user that enters the system (Armstrong, 2006). To that end, network effects describe the "effect of one user on the consumption value realized by other users" (Wildman, 2006, p. 78), shaping demand interdependencies. The classic example of the network effect is the telephone – useless to a single user alone, but exponentially useful the more users join the network. When networks grow, it creates direct positive network effects, expanding the value of the service. This affects weaker networks negatively, creating winner-takes-all markets (Fjell et al., 2010). Indirect positive network effects are attained when complementary products enhance the number of users, for instance how answering machines created indirect network effects from the telephone (Wildman, 2006). Digital platforms thus have powerful network effects, linking content with users, in turn attracting complementary products.

Because platforms engender economies of scale, they exert power and influence in the network, and thus have a tendency towards concentration (McChesney, 2013, p. 132). Platforms are essentially bottlenecks for scarce and valuable resources and act as gatekeepers who filter, select, accumulate, process and package content, leading to lock-in – a process whereby companies become dependent on a particular platform. Lock-in creates high switching costs to a competing service provider, not least because of high compatibility pressures, and raises barriers to entry (Cunningham et al., 2015). A key to platforms is that they need to design their price structure to bring both parties on board (Rochet & Tirole, 2006). Moreover, success on either side of the market depends on good performance on the other. This principle explains the detrimental effects of the loss of the advertising market for news media. With lower success on the audience market, the platform loses value on the advertising side. Moreover, as the news needs to go where the audience is, search and social media effectively assume the networking power that news media used to have in the past (this problem will be dealt with in more detail in Chapter 5).

Not all advertisers aim for mass audiences, however. While a large supermarket chain may target the general consumer, producers of more specialised, high-end, or exclusive goods may want to target more specific consumer groups, such as high-income cosmopolitans living in large cities. The concept of differentiation applies here, as products can be tailored towards more target audiences (Conboy & Steel, 2009). Product differentiation is the primary means by which media companies compete (Hollifield, 2006). Companies differentiate their goods to meet the diversity of tastes in consumers (Perloff & Salop, 1985). Arguably, differentiation loses some of its power in AI markets. In programmatic advertising, the context in which advertising is displayed matters less than reaching the right user in the right use situation. While some attention has been brought on the extent to which programmatic advertising ignores the content context in which advertising is displayed (leading to grim examples of brands such as IBM and Microsoft displayed alongside contentious content, for instance on YouTube (Garrahan, 2017; Nicas, 2017), and thus presenting potential harm to the brand), the news environment has lost some of its attraction to advertisers, not least because of readership decline (Newman et al., 2021). Differentiation to suit the advertising side of the market therefore has less meaning in news markets where users can be reached through multiple platforms, particularly platforms like Google and Facebook that people use every day. In fact, what differentiates news providers in the programmatic advertising market has more to do with their audience data and analytical power than the types of audiences they reach.

The product characteristics of journalism could be seen as a strength in this new competitive situation, however. While news markets are markets with highly similar products (McCombs, 1988, p. 130), no two news products are perfect substitutes (Litman, 1988). The concept of substitutes refers to the extent to which there is an alternative available offer in the market. News can be found everywhere, but no two news stories are the same, even when the topic is the same. The prerequisite for this principle is, however, editorial treatment. Conglomeration often leads to syndication of content, mandated wire copy or news agency use, and centralised production of generic content in the lifestyle, sports, and entertainment genres (Hendrickx, 2020; Sjøvaag, 2014a; Soloski, 1989). Such efficiency tactics can lead to an increased homogenisation of content, lowering the substitution rate within the industry. What remains difficult to substitute, however, is local information. To that end, local newspapers still have non-substitutability characteristics on the content side. What is substitutable in the local news markets, however, is audience reach, which increases the competition from Google and Facebook on the advertising side of the market.

Substitution is nevertheless a prerequisite for competition – the presence of similar products with similar utilities for a similar price (Hollifield, 2006). Goods have utility if they satisfy consumer needs or desires (Berg et al., 2013). Utility thus refers to the benefit that individual consumers perceive to derive from products or services (Wildman, 2006). These characteristics make defining the competitive landscape difficult for media companies, both in terms of what products they compete with and the geographical market of competition. As people also derive different utility from different media products, establishing the substitutability of media products can be tricky (Lacy, 2004). News outlets no longer just compete with other news outlets for advertising revenue, they compete with the entire tech industry (Krebs et al., 2021). Moreover, they compete with other types of media for users' time, attention, and money. Here, competition for audiences reflects how the competitive context also extends to the kind of user data that can enable news organisations to develop their products, improve their attractiveness to advertisers, and develop strategies for the future.

Because daily news offers similar products, their substitution rate is high. Breaking, general news, can be found everywhere. For more specialised content, such as local news, substitution is low. Product differentiation is used in such markets to create niches to reduce substitution. Newspapers have historically differentiated themselves along the lines of quality, location, and editorial orientation, but newspapers also need to remain substitutes in order to compete within the general circulation market. Differentiation also entails rising costs, especially in markets with many similar products and low entry barriers (Litman, 1988). The strategy of differentiation has been challenged by the role of social media in news dissemination and discovery. Within the Facebook environment, for instance, it is difficult to differentiate news products, as every news story looks the same. The online environment thus effectively serves to un-differentiate journalistic products (Haim et al., 2021; Munger, 2020). A number of recent trends thus arguably serve to decrease the potential of differentiation strategies in news markets. Phenomena like fake news and content marketing that assume the form of news (Ferrer Conill, 2016), and news automation and 'robot' journalism (Lindén, 2017) that capitalise on news language standardisation all serve to 'flatten' the differentiation space in which news can operate. On the other hand, audience analytics (Ferrucci, 2020) promotes strategic differentiation in the content that reaches individual end-users (Hendrickx et al., 2021), to the extent that differentiation moves from the production end to the consumption end of the value chain.

Rather than applying costly differentiation strategies, then, newspapers have historically tended to target mass, general audiences by bundling different news products together. Bundles create economic advantages because they reduce the cost of production and allow for standardisation (Porter, 1985), particularly in the technology needed for production. It also simplifies consumer orientation and reduces marketing costs (Crawford, 2008). When products are bundled together, companies can charge higher prices for the collective product than they would be able to charge for individual items. Customers are also generally more willing to pay for a combination of products than individual products (Kammer et al., 2015; Stahl & Maass, 2004). The printed newspaper is a 'bundle' that consists of many types of content designed to satisfy a range of consumer tastes. The web infrastructure allowed news organisations to bundle off content into separate sections, allowing users to circumvent content they at least had to flip past in the printed edition, reducing the public good quality of news. The concept of the bundle has taken on further meaning in the world of social media. A news story on Facebook contains not only the story itself, but also social information about its popularity and response (Munger, 2020), increasing the scope of what a news story can potentially bundle.

The features that provide news with competitive advantage – its non-rivalrous nature, its bundled products, its network effect linking advertisers with audiences, and its public good characteristic – all face challenges in the switch to AI. The platform takeover of newspapers' network effect has therefore not only created a new economic environment in which journalism must operate. It also challenges the cost structure of the news industries themselves, and their business models.

The cost structure of news

Newspapers comprise a range of enterprises including news gathering, ad sales, printing, and distribution. Edge (2019) has thus described newspapers as "deceptively complex economic commodities" (p. 20). The production of media products has high fixed costs and low variable costs. It is expensive to produce the first copy, but inexpensive to make more copies of the original. The more copies that can be sold from the original, the lower the unit cost, which allows companies to lower prices, benefiting the consumer. The organisation of journalism itself is expensive. Office space, staff, technology, printing, distribution, and administration constitute high expenses. The cost structure of a printed newspaper therefore means that newspaper markets have high barriers to entry. Barriers to entry not only refers to the price of getting started, but also to access to strategic resources, such as labour, patents, or rights (Litman, 1988). Hence, in the pre-internet era, starting up was expensive. Web production means that a lot of the costs associated with getting the product to the consumer – printing facilities and technology, paper and ink, and trucks and drivers for distribution – can be taken out of the equation. However, it turns out that digital journalism, while it does save money on the distribution side – about 30 percent, according to Hardy (2017a) – does not necessarily reduce the cost of making news (Picard, 2017; Ryfe, 2021). Hindman (2018) has, in fact, argued that internet distribution can also be seen as costly when all the technology and labour that goes into site and app design, user engagement features, personalisation, advertising, and search engine optimising are factored in. Hence, journalism still has relatively high fixed costs (Nielsen, 2016).

Industries with high entry barriers and high fixed costs – costs that are constant – are characterised by economies of scale and scope. Economies of scale explains the advantages of large production, while economies of scope explains the advantages of producing multiple products – both meaning lower cost per unit. Scale economies exist where "the cost of providing an extra unit of a good falls as the scale of output expands" (Doyle, 2013, p. 15). The more copies produced, the less the cost of each subsequent copy. For digital media, scale also entails an increase in value (Ryfe, 2021), as data collection on user interaction increases content targeting. To that end, the technology of distribution networks has significantly raised the scale potential of products (Noam, 2018). Economies of scope means that savings and efficiency can be attained by using the same inputs to produce more than one product, or by repackaging or repurposing content to other markets (Cunningham et al., 2015). Large companies tend to attain low unit cost because they can afford more specialised technologies, they have pricing power when dealing with suppliers, and they can borrow money more cheaply. Attaining size is therefore cost effective, which leads to another characteristic of media markets – concentration.

Markets can be either perfect competition markets, monopolistic competition markets, oligopolies, or monopolies. Perfect competition means that no firm can have market power. Cunningham et al. (2015) have used websites as an example of perfect competition markets where there are multiple sellers, homogenous products, easy substitution, and strong price competition. However, perfectly competitive markets are generally unrealistic because industries tend to concentrate. Monopolistic competitive markets are markets that produce similar products, but not perfect substitutes (Wildman, 2006). Monopolistic competition markets are often populated by many firms and thus characterised by an excess in production and differentiated products. Media markets that display monopolistic competition include book publishing, magazines, radio, and national newspapers (Cunningham et al., 2015). Oligopolies are markets with only a couple of dominant players. Oligopoly markets are populated by a relatively small number of firms that sell similar products. In the media industries this includes the markets for music recording, film, television, and web search (ibid.). Monopoly markets are markets where one company has total market power, or there is only one supplier of the product (Flew, 2012). Monopoly markets can therefore be expected to lead to high economic performance but not necessarily the best quality (Hollifield, 2006). In Western media markets, telecommunication sectors tend to be monopolies (Picard & Dal Zotto, 2016).

Monopoly markets are a concern when it comes to media products because of an implied threat, namely that monopoly on content may also mean a monopoly of ideas (Ruotolo, 1988). The association between monopoly power and homogeneity of content is a contentious one, but nevertheless one that has sticky properties. It makes sense, somehow, to think that monopoly media ownership can have an adverse effect on the diversity of ideas in the public sphere. There is evidence, however, that monopoly media, where one owner controls the entire market, tend to differentiate their products to satisfy a wider range of audience tastes. Having complete control of the market, and with no rivals to substitute, monopoly players can target multiple groups without the risk of rivals (cf. Berry & Waldfogel, 2001). Noam (2009) has noted that the fear of media monopoly is not just born out of historical examples of moguls exercising their ownership power, with potential effects on politics or the public discourse. People also tend to blame the media for a range of social problems, including violence, racism, bias, and stereotyping. Concluding that the negative effects of media are a direct consequence of media concentration is, however, contentious. It is just as likely, notes Noam (ibid., p. 13), that the exploitation of market power for political influence, as well as socially adverse content, is a result of profit orientation rather than market structure.

While the move to online news production and dissemination has led to savings in the news industries, there is a limit to how much companies can reduce the cost of making news. During periods of intense saving strategies in the newspaper sector, notably during the financial crises of 2008 and 2012, many jobs in journalism were lost. However, jobs are usually the last expense news companies want to reduce. That is, they tend to look for savings elsewhere before they tackle the product itself. In these periods of belt-tightening, newspapers have usually sold off property, centralised management functions, and increased efficiency in content production before they cut staff. As economies of scale and scope facilitate such measures, news industries went through processes of consolidation in these periods. Since advertising began to migrate towards the tech platforms after the switch to AI around 2014–2015, newspapers have essentially employed the same tactic – looking for scale and scope advantages to continue producing news at lower costs. Part of the problem that journalism faces here of course is that the business model for news has come under severe pressure in the platform economy.

Journalism's business model

There have been many attempts to define the business model for news. They tend to defy clear agreement in the literature (cf. von Rimscha, 2016). They are often used colloquially to denote how a company makes money (Evens, 2018), or the creation, realisation, and delivery of economic value (Cook & Sirkkunen, 2013; Hess & Waller, 2017; Holm et al., 2013). However, Picard (2017) asserts that we need to distinguish between a firm's business model and its funding model. Here, the funding model is how a business makes money, comprising its income and revenue. A business model, on the other hand, includes a company's business logics, its value proposition, its processes and relationships, and its customer relations (Picard, 2011). A business model mobilises both revenue and strategy. Hence, a business model seeks to describe not just how value is created, but how it is captured (Zott et al., 2011). Resources are therefore key to business models, as they are about both creating and capturing value (von Rimscha, 2016). Delivering this value relies on the internal processes of the firm, and its network of partners for creating, marketing, and delivering value to generate value streams and profit (Holm et al., 2013). The business model of traditional media has always been to extract revenues from advertisers in return for delivering audiences to them. In this model, much of the cost is carried by the advertisers, payment models are based on aggregating a large consumer base, and the product is based on standardisation (Küng, 2017). It is therefore not difficult to see how journalism's business model has been challenged by digital disruption. Not only have advertising substitutes diminished; the consumer base has also become more fragmented, and standardised products have become less valuable in the digital economy.

A business model relies to varying degrees on a company's surrounding markets – the consumers who buy their products and competitors that compete for consumers and other resources. Consumer markets are in turn shaped by the nature of demand, willingness to pay among consumers, and the level of differentiation needed to suit consumer tastes. The presence of competitors thus shapes the structure of the sales market and the behaviour of existing and potential customers (von Rimscha, 2016). Media companies also rely on the procurement market for the supply of products and services for content and distribution. Hence, central to a competitive business strategy is choosing in which product market to compete, how to compete, which resources to deploy, how to distribute costs, and how to attain advantages through differentiation strategies (Varadarajan & Yadav, 2009). With the expansion of the digital economy, many of these 'choices' are no longer available to news organisations. News may be one particular product market that shapes company strategies, but news is not just in competition with other news. This is an attention market after all, and journalism must compete with all other types of content for the time and attention of audiences. Moreover, the competitive space has expanded, particularly the competition for advertising. Hence, the concept of a business model, or how the news media is able to capture value, is challenged precisely because the markets have changed.

Critiques against the business model framework emphasise its failure to recognise externalities – the value beyond the product itself (Picard, 2002). The problem with business models, says von Rimscha (2016), is that they tend to reduce media to a business that makes money with media. The business model for news also presents itself differently whether we are talking about an analogue market situation, an online market, or a market characterised by AI technology. In the analogue era, the two-sided business model was based on large audiences, low costs, and high advertising income (Picard, 2009b). This meant high entry barriers, effective economies of scale, monopoly power in individual markets, and centralised production and distribution (Mensing, 2007). As Franklin (2008) has noted, this business model "simply does not translate to online news" (p. 25).

In fact, the platform ecology in which journalism operates today is more correctly characterised as multi-sided markets, where platforms bring together multiple end-users and where most of the income comes from one side (Evans, 2003; Helmond, 2015). The traditional media value chain and business model is based on supply-side economics, which entails high fixed costs and low variable costs, decreasing unit cost with scale and monopoly concentration. Conversely, the demand-side economics that characterises multi-sided markets relies on strong network effects where external forces create value rather than depleting them (Van Alstyne et al., 2016). To that end, the two-sided market model is severely challenged by the characteristics of platform economics, where content developers such as news organisations no longer have control over production and distribution, but rather become dispensable (Nieborg & Poell, 2018).

Throughout the digital transformation, however, research has continued to rely on the two-sided market model (e.g., Choi & Yang, 2021; Chatterjee & Zhou, 2021). As news media shifted to the online realm in the first wave of digitalisation, research tended to focus on business models as the multiplication of distribution channels (Holm et al., 2013) and revenue streams (Berte & De Bens, 2009); diversification, synergies, and cross-media strategies (Carvajal and Avilés, 2008); speed and experimentation (Chaharbaghi et al., 2003); and innovation and entrepreneurialism (Varadarajan et al., 2008). The online market was characterised by low entry barriers, intense competition, lower fixed costs, and decentralised production and distribution. As news businesses began to employ models for an electronic reality, it did not change business models all that much (cf. Mensing, 2007), largely because traditional economic principles still held true. When studying the business models of 42 publishers in the early 2000s, WAN-IFRA (2006) found future challenges to amount to market predictability, decreased return on investment, rising technology costs, and restrictions on credit. Attaining first-mover advantages became important, as did cooperation and alliance building. Coupled with product innovation, the first-mover advantage should ideally secure audience retention (Varadarajan et al., 2008). However, as the power shifted to the consumer, the network aspect became more important to gain access to new markets (cf. Chaharbaghi et al., 2003).

Whereas the WAN-IFRA report (2006) asserts that established economic principles still held in this period, Chaharbaghi and colleagues (2003) have argued the opposite, as "the key assumption that growth and brand building are the most important business objectives turned out to be invalid" (p. 387). Traditional media struggled to find sustainable business models in the switch to online, which led them to reduce the scale and scope of their operations to save on expenses. Balancing old and new activities became costly and difficult, which put many newspapers into a defender position (Krumsvik, 2014). This was largely because many news organisations were reluctant to change their business model (Evens, 2018). This was not only because organisations are generally characterised by inertia, but also because media companies had to adapt with scarcer resources (Küng, 2011). As van der Wurff (2005) found when studying the online news market in the Netherlands in the early 2000s, incumbents' online strategies were mainly reactive, often triggered by new entrants, but hampered by a lack of resources. Chyi (2013) has described this as a "suicidal spiral", where the belief in the ultimate death of the printed product led newspapers to cut resources, which led to a further decline in circulation and advertising revenue, eventually killing the core product. Such a rapid decline in income hindered newspapers' flexibility to adapt in a changing market situation. It became difficult to cover the large costs of running a general news business, which led newspapers to scale down their operations, and shift costs to consumers (Picard, 2009a, p. 3).

The second wave of digitalisation, the switch to AI, saw a turn towards more integrated and adapted business models. Here, the funding of journalism has shifted from advertisers to users (Olsen et al., 2021). Monetisation strategies in this period have thus focused on maximising revenue from customers who are willing to pay (Hardy, 2017b), and targeting elite or specialist audiences with scarce, high-value content through enhanced cross-platform availability (Hardy, 2017a; Wirtz & Elsäßer, 2017). Newspaper companies have also begun focusing more on portfolio diversification (Sjøvaag & Owren, 2021b) – moving into market segments that are not already occupied by direct competitors (Evens, 2018). Legacy media have thus started creating vertical services alongside the core news business, including digital marketing services, events, commercial printing, and business-to-business publishing (Lehtisaari et al., 2018).

However, Cawley (2019) has found that considerable resources are still used to manage the print product in the U.K., suggesting that digital transformations are still occurring in operational contexts anchored in print managerial logics and behaviours. To that end, Küng (2017) asserts that the key challenge for news at this point is organisational. Media companies have, therefore, been more or less constantly restructuring their operations for the last 20–30 years. Organisational models in the online phase shifted towards flat hierarchies (Chaharbaghi et al., 2003) and convergent newsrooms (Singer, 2004; Tameling & Broersma, 2013) to facilitate more innovation (Brüggemann et al., 2016), entrepreneurialism (Pavlik, 2013), adaptation (Küng, 2011), and diversification (Carvajal & Avilés, 2008, p. 329) in newsrooms. As institutions tend to be path dependent, this also led to mimicry and trend following in news innovation efforts in this period, largely explaining why efforts towards convergent newsrooms, multimedia technology, and interactive technologies sometimes came across as rather half-hearted attempts (Lowrey, 2012). As Nielsen (2016) has noted, organisational change is difficult for journalism. Moreover, while effective transformations require good organisations, Küng (2017) has observed that actually being good organisations was never a priority for media companies.

In the AI phase, companies have focused more on increasing efficiency and optimal resource utilisation over newsroom restructuring. This includes the centralisation of product and process development (Lehtisaari et al., 2018), an orientation towards dynamic capabilities (cf. Ekberg 2020), a heightened focus on continuous transformational change (Kosterich, 2020), and a turn to more value-oriented media management (Altmeppen et al., 2017). Part of this turn is a drive towards developing more adaptive start-up cultures in the newsroom itself (Kosterich & Weber, 2018). To that end, Küng (2017) asserts that many media companies have abandoned strategy altogether in favour of innovation and tactical moves. The challenge here is that multiple processes are often taking place at once, with different speeds and with counterfactual data on which to base those tactical decisions. The expanded competitive landscape in which news organisations must manoeuvre also provides new challenges. Technology companies are well funded, which means they can afford to fail. In this rapidly shifting landscape, the news media are not really funded to afford the kind of failure that inevitably comes with innovation. In fact, organisational developments in journalism are increasingly characterised by enabling integration between the news and technology industries (Kosterich, 2020; Kosterich & Weber, 2019). News organisations are adjusting their business models to the platform economy, which in turn impacts on their organisational strategies.

Advertising

Journalism's main problem in today's news market is that it has lost its key competitive advantage as the platform connecting advertisers with their desired demographics. While news media's dependence on advertising remains high, advertisers' need for news media has reduced to the point where it has never been smaller. Advertisers no longer seek the positive association of editorial products (Braun & Eklund, 2019), largely because they no longer need to. Advertising investments have shifted to Google for search advertising, Facebook for mobile advertising, and YouTube for digital video advertising. To that end, Feng and Ots (2018) note that there are increasing ambiguities about how to properly define advertising and advertising markets.

The advertising industry is often described as adaptable (ibid.). Advertisers were quick to respond to the possibilities offered by the internet. Online advertising did not look that dissimilar from traditional printed advertising in the beginning. While they adopted traditional forms online, such as banner and display advertising, online advertising also developed affordances that ultimately engendered new formats and business models. Clickable display ads combined traditional and interactive forms in a way that transformed the understanding of audiences from exposure to action. Online advertising thus developed new approaches to reach consumers, detached from content (Wang, 2018). However, there is also some contention about the effectiveness of online ads. Many of these formats are seen as intrusive and annoying, to which the advertising industry responded – first, with pop-ups and animations, triggering even more negative consumer responses, and secondly, with native advertising, designed to embed more seamlessly with content.

Whether characterised as native advertising or branded content, this form of advertising is marketing's response to banner blindness, advertising fatigue, and ad blocking (Feng & Ots, 2018). Native advertising includes sponsored social media posts, sponsored hyperlinks, and article-style native content (Harms et al., 2019). In a news media context, native advertising is 'in-stream' content – advertising integration without editorial separation (Hardy, 2017b). Ferrer-Conill (2016) defines native advertising as 'a form of paid content marketing, adopting the form and function of editorial content with the attempt to recreate the user experience of reading news instead of advertising content' (p. 905). To that end, native advertising is marketing's 'resort to journalism logic and practices' (Feng & Ots, 2018, p. 157), where the brand is the central character of the story. Moreover, the organisation of native advertising differs from traditional ad work.

Advertising markets used to be tied to the structure of news markets in various countries, differing along national (e.g., in the U.K.), regional (e.g., in Germany) and local (e.g., in the U.S.) news market structures (Picard, 2008). Hence, the advertising 'currency' that news media held was reach, which segmented markets geographically (Ohlsson & Facht, 2017). In analogue markets, horizontal organisation was beneficial because it allowed news companies to control advertising in adjacent markets. As advertisers preferred geographic segmentation (Krumsvik & Sundet, 2011), this gave many local newspapers near monopoly (Picard, 2018), reflecting in large part an absence in competition. Moreover, the two-sided business model was also premised on advertisers' preference for a limited number of providers, which allowed monopolist players to charge high prices for advertising space. The umbrella model of newspaper publishing explains how advertising used to work in these markets (Rosse, 1975). The umbrella model was initially used to describe the intra-layer, or geographic, competition among newspapers in metropolitan American markets. Competition here consisted of four layers (Lacy, 1988) – metropolitan dailies providing regional coverage, suburban dailies, national papers, and weekly newspapers. In this model, a newspaper would produce unique, non-substitutable products – local information – ensuring it could operate without direct competition within its layer, handling the reader and advertiser needs in its geographic area (Bridges et al., 2002).

Programmatic advertising introduces competition in the local advertising market, causing the umbrella model to crumble (Sjøvaag & Owren, 2021a). Local papers are not as competitive in this market. Marketing decisions are no longer made at the local level, due in large part to the chainification of retail. Advertising used to be an isolated practice based on dyadic and personal agency–client relationships between the staff at the marketing department of local newspapers and local merchants (Feng & Ots, 2018). Whereas advertising decisions were once made locally, they are now increasingly made centrally by advertising agencies. Advertisers pay for direct access to the consumer online, circumventing the platform function that news industries used to provide. Much of this advertising is also driven by price customisation, or dynamic pricing. Rather than selling audiences 'in bulk', dynamic pricing means charging different prices to different customers, using algorithmic profiling, targeting audiences based on clicks, transaction history and third-party user information (Bodó, 2019), and even factors such as geography, time, and temperature (Park, 2017). Current competitive advantage in the advertising market is thus data-driven rather than reach-driven (Ohlsson & Facht, 2017).

This turn towards programmatic advertising has disrupted the advertising ecosystem. The market has shifted from local to national, from news to search and social, and towards global networks. Nevertheless, many newspapers have continued to rely on advertising as their main source of revenue (cf. Cawley, 2019). Nielsen (2016) thus sees only two options for newspapers trying to retain their status as advertising platforms in this disruption, either differentiation or scale (see also Ryfe, 2021). Adapting to this shift means that publishers have begun to personalise news based on user profiles relying on clicks, transaction history, and third-party user information (Bodó, 2019; Harms et al., 2019). This advertising strategy focuses on short-term interaction over long-term brand awareness. This stands in direct opposition to the established logic of news operations, which is to generate long-term brand loyalty. As advertising is essential to the business model of news, the altered logics of the advertising industry and the introduction of competitive markets in this realm change the very meaning of advertising for the news industries. Journalism is no longer in a unique position to offer valuable audiences, and the brand matters less. The loss of advertising income thus entails the largest disruption to journalism's business model, the basis for which is a change in the technology linking the two sides of the market.

Disruptions and transformations in the news industries

Disruption is a keyword that was mobilised frequently in research on the first wave of the digitalisation of the news industries. Technology change can alter what drives cost in an industry. It is also one of the main drivers of competition (Porter, 1985). Whereas in the analogue model, technology limited competition, internet technology is a common advantage, available to all (Noam, 2009). In a nutshell, the internet lowered barriers to entry, simplified production, lowered marginal costs, and increased competition and the speed of innovation, leading to higher scale economics. McDowell (2011) thus asserts that the internet is what made the news a commodity. The online disruption meant news media had to start thinking about how they make money.

Clayton Christensen (1997) has described disruption as a change caused by technology that is so revolutionary that it threatens the leaders of an existing market, making certain skills obsolete in the process. Christensen (2003) later replaced 'technology' with 'innovation', to emphasise that it is innovators rather than technology that disrupt (cf. Nee, 2013). Despite Christensen's refocus on innovation, disruption in the news industries is still largely thought of as technological (e.g., Meyer, 2009), or more precisely – digital (Maijanen et al., 2019). Here, Chyi (2013) has rather effectively criticised the industry's adoption of Christensen's disruption/innovation thesis. The mistake that newspapers made here, Chyi asserts (ibid.), is that the news industries believed digital formats would replace the physical format. Instead, newsprint has proven to be quite persistent (Brüggemann et al., 2016; Chyi & Tenenboim, 2019b). This has left newspapers in a perpetual crisis mode – preparing for a digital-only future while still holding on to the printed product.

This perpetual crisis mode illustrates the extent to which disruption is not an event but a process – one that can take years (Karimi & Walter, 2015). When Brüggemann and colleagues (2016) looked into newspapers' response to this crisis, they found that news organisations were generally more concerned with preventing future problems than they were with dealing with the one at hand. They also found that news organisations' innovation measures tended to resort to old business models. For instance, European newspapers began calling for better framework conditions from the state, essentially lobbying for increased state subsidies to sustain their operations. Scandinavian news media have also re-introduced the subscription model from the print era (Olsen et al., 2021), and many newspapers have worked hard to re-train audiences to pay for news. This turn towards established business model thinking thus signals the extent to which newspapers are planning for a future based primarily on audience revenue (cf. Lehtisaari et al., 2018).

What is gone, what remains

Despite the disruption that digitisation and AI presents to journalism's business model, key features of journalism's organisation persist. The fundamental tenets of news remain intact. Journalism is still, at its core, a public good with non-rivalrous and non-excludable characteristics. At least it has the potential to be. Subscription and membership models do raise the barriers to news for people who do not have the means or willingness to pay for quality news. The proliferation of misinformation on social media platforms certainly contributes to reduce the quality of information and the general trust in news as an institution, but journalism nevertheless still has positive externalities that encourage democracy, promote transparency, and discourage corruption (cf. Becker et al., 2009).

Threats to journalism's ability to fulfil this social welfare function include not only the toxic online information environments that diminish trust in news, native advertising blurring the lines between commercial and editorial messages, and the platforms that siphon off advertising revenue – market failure is still very much a threat to news as a product. Because, as Nielsen (2016) remarks, people are more willing to waste their time than their money, their gravitation towards free content is also a direct reflection of the market failure risks associated with merit goods. News media calls for state support therefore reflect more than a search for sustainable and predictable income streams. As news media turn to the state for economic support this also illustrates the enduring belief that the news industries actually have in the public good characteristics of their product – that it is indeed worthy of state support. Journalism is a public good, the externality value of which is essential for a well-functioning public conversation, public oversight, and democratic processes. When the markets fail to provide the necessary income to sustain such a merit good, governments should step in to make sure the sector is sustainable. In many countries, governments have been quite receptive to this normative argument by the news lobby. At least in the Nordic countries, where state support continues to enjoy broad political support across party lines (Sjøvaag, 2019). Hence, while the public good quality of journalism may be in question concerning how the content and function of news may be conceptualised, the principle still carries normative merits, with political effectiveness.

Journalism's business model, while severely disrupted, thus continues to rely on two-sided market logics. Business model innovation, as such, tends to resort to a combination of existing and emerging income streams, a return to subscription being key to many newspapers' funding models. Branding is therefore still important to news industries' marketing strategies, as audience conversion is necessary to build attractive and predictable target groups for journalism's remaining advertisers (Olsen et al., 2021). While the existence of an advertising market as such is very much in question, the news brand seems to attain higher value to audiences, as well as to marketers, in times of crisis. This not only pertains to the coronavirus pandemic, which saw people return to trusted news brands for reliable news (Newman et al., 2021). Programmatic advertising has also shown serious flaws in its adjacency logics – overlooking the value, or conversely, the risk – of the context in which ads are placed. The effectiveness of social media advertising has also been questioned, not least because of overload and spam (Noam, 2018), reflecting, again, advertising's tendency to overlook the relevance of context, and the value that users place on their own control over when and how to engage with advertising content (cf. Berte & De Bens, 2009). There might still be a chance, then, for journalism to capitalise on the trusted brand of news as 'low-risk' spaces for information consumption. This, however, depends on the extent to which news is actually able to reach consumers, who are now increasingly reliant on third-party intermediaries in the platform ecology.

The platform function that news used to have in connecting advertisers with audiences – and the positive externalities resulting from this function – is all but gone, assumed by digital giants like Facebook, Google, Amazon, and YouTube. Platforms tend to subsidise one group of users. Newspapers used to extend this subsidy to its readers, selling the product below production cost, subsidised by the advertising side (Rieder & Sire, 2014). Digital intermediaries have upset this model to the point where newspapers also sell advertising below production cost. It seems that news media have two options to respond to this reality. They can either accept that they are, in fact, still in the advertising business and realise they have lost to platforms and move into a low cost/low margins business, or they need to plan for a future without advertising revenue and build multiple revenue streams with smaller revenue but larger margins (Bell et al., 2017). Publishers have found it difficult, however, to choose a strategy here, and tend to optimise for both scenarios.

To the extent that news media are able to retain some part of the platform function in the media ecology, scale has become imperative. Both for programmatic advertising and audience analytics, scale is important. To that end, chain ownership must be said to be one of the more enduring and indeed increasingly important organisational features of journalistic production for sustaining what remains of the two-sided business model for news. Chains allow advertisers to coordinate campaigns on a large scale through central marketing departments. Chains also allow news managers to maximise data collection and thus increase the power of their audience analytics. The scale economies that chains afford also increase the efficiency of the organisation, centralise management, enable technology investment and innovation, and foster better resource utilisation on the content side. Scale therefore means significant competitive advantage on both sides of the dual market, extending the relevance of the two-sided business model. Rather than adjusting to a future without advertising revenue, chain formation allows newspapers to retain significance through scale. This is particularly relevant in regions where certain umbrella market characteristics remain, like in Scandinavia, with strong local newspaper structures and monopolistic markets that allow chains to control large market segments.

Many scholars have characterised these enduring forms of journalism's organisation as inertia (Evens, 2018; Küng, 2017), reflecting a dangerous lack of adaptability to the new ecology. Disappointing as this lack of leanness may be, perhaps this inertia also suggests that there is a certain source of strength embedded in journalism's long-standing organisational features. In the mid-to-late 2000s, scholars were forceful in their calls for entrepreneurialism in journalism – envisioning newsroom-less futures where the news was produced by freelance reporters, each with their own blog updated from home (cf. Deuze, 2008). Scholars also called for news media to look to Google (e.g., Jarvis, 2009), to lean more on audience contributors through 'produsage' (Bruns, 2010), and to open up their newsrooms to user generated content (cf. Singer, 2010). Particularly in the U.S., scholars have been optimistic about new ownership and funding models for journalism in the form of trusts and foundations (Lewis, 2011). As it turns out, none of these models for ownership and production are very sustainable, at least on their own. Perhaps this reflects institutional resistance on the part of journalism itself. It is more likely, however, that the enduring forms of journalism's organisation – the two-sided business model, the chain ownership formation, and the newsroom itself, provide the institutional stability that journalism needs as it adjusts to a new normal – a normal in which the markets for news have slimmed down significantly, and where competition has increased incrementally.

In the next chapter, we analyse what this move towards larger organisational units means for journalism, by looking at trends towards ownership concentration in the Scandinavian news industries.

3 Market concentration

Media ownership is concentrating in the Nordics. Large, dominant regional chain corporations such as Amedia, Polaris, and Bonnier have, since 2017–2018, moved in to acquire mid-sized companies, increasing their holdings. At the same time, independent local newspapers are seeking corporate ownership. Local newspaper structures are, moreover, consolidating across Scandinavian borders. For local newspapers, corporate ownership presents as a solution to gain access to the digital infrastructures needed to link up to the digital economy, particularly in the advertising markets. They also need the sophisticated data analytics tools developed by larger players to gain insight into their digital audiences, necessary for digital subscription conversion. Corporate consolidation in Scandinavian newspaper markets thus presents the necessary scale and scope needed for local news structures to survive the switch to a digital economy in local, monopolistic markets. Most acquisitions are also amicable affairs, welcomed by both parties. And while policy and regulation seem to be adjusting to the mutual will to corporatisation by previously independently owned operations, concerns are also raised regarding the future risks posed by a super-consolidated regional news landscape. Whether or not this concentration presents a step towards market failure, local journalism is facing this disruption by turning to chain formations – one of the enduring forms of journalism.

Scandinavian newspaper markets

Scandinavia is located in the north of Europe and comprises Denmark, Norway, and Sweden. The region has about 20 million inhabitants. The countries rank in the top four on the press freedom index (Reporters Without Borders, 2021), together with Finland, and in the top seven in the UN's Democracy Index (2020). The countries have similar political systems, with parliamentary, representative, democratic constitutional monarchy. They also share a cultural history, with similar languages (Sjøvaag, 2019). Their

DOI: 10.4324/9781003081791-3

media systems are part of the Northern cluster (Brüggemann et al., 2014) of democratic corporatist media systems (Hallin & Mancini, 2004), characterised as media welfare states (Syvertsen et al., 2014). Welfare states are based on redistribution of wealth, built around universalism and social security (Esping-Andersen, 1990). The Scandinavian welfare states are thus designed to shield individuals from the negative effects of market and class mechanisms for which market intervention is a commonly used tool (Kammer, 2016). Their political and economic systems are characterised by many small corporations with local affiliations, strong rational-legal authority (Ihlen et al., 2015) and consensus politics (Hjarvard & Kammer, 2015). These are corporate systems with strong interest group organisation, institutionalised processes of bargaining, and informal coordination, and generally have low levels of political conflict. Political systems are, however, more concentrated in Denmark and Sweden than in Norway, where centre-periphery conflicts are stronger, largely explained by higher dispersal in demographic and geographical power.

Scandinavian governments are active in structuring media markets. Public support exists for local and niche newspapers to sustain journalism in local and competitive markets. Government support is non-political, secured through arm's-length principles of governance (Engelstad et al., 2017). That is, press support is distributed through politically independent authorities. All three countries have strong, popular, public service media sustained by state funding in mixed broadcasting systems alongside successful commercial competition (Ohlsson & Sjøvaag, 2019). Their media systems include laws that protect editorial freedom, self-regulatory oversight, and direct and indirect public funding, the aims of which are to secure pluralism and competition. Direct funding is provided to public service media, local and niche news outlets. News organisations are also exempt from VAT. Media ownership falls under the purview of general competition law, but the Ministries of Media and Culture have monitoring powers in questions of ownership transparency.

Communication infrastructures are seen as public goods – a principle that was established in the analogue era, and which has path-dependent effects on the media system, sustaining established and incumbent media (Syvertsen et al., 2014). Newspaper readership remains high, mostly sustained by paid subscription, and Scandinavian audiences also have comparatively high willingness-to-pay for digital news products. Scandinavian news audiences have relatively high trust in news and public service media, while local and regional newspapers continue to enjoy the highest trust among news sources in these countries. According to Reuters Digital News Report (Newman et al., 2021), the proportion of audiences that pay for news is 16 percent in Denmark, 30 percent in Sweden, and 45 percent in Norway.

Trust in news overall is 50 percent in Sweden, 57 percent in Norway and 59 percent in Denmark. However, the media welfare state is not without its challenges. Public service media are facing increasing restrictions from regulators based on sustaining commercial media (Sjøvaag, Pedersen & Owren, 2019), and advertising expenditure has shifted towards Facebook and Google (Ohlsson & Facht, 2017).

The Scandinavian newspaper markets are decentralised and comparatively abundant. The majority of newspapers are local in distribution and profile (Sjøvaag, Pedersen & Lægreid, 2019). Local newspaper ownership has historically been more diverse than at the regional and national levels, contributing to external pluralism in the media systems. All three countries have, however, seen a consolidation in local newspaper structures since the shift to AI. Localism is a more predominant trait in the Norwegian and Swedish media systems than it is in Denmark (Fletcher & Nielsen, 2017), explained in large part by differences in geography and political structure. Strong incumbent positions have also enabled established news organisations to retain dominant positions in digital markets (Sjøvaag, Stavelin et al., 2019). Communication infrastructures were digitised early in this region, which allowed market leaders to innovate on the base of high revenues (Ottosen & Krumsvik, 2012; Slaatta, 2015). This, in turn, gave an advantage to already dominant national media. Paywall penetration is high, with more than half of newspapers in the region having some sort of subscription model for online content (Sjøvaag, 2019).

The newspaper structure consists of four types of newspapers (cf. ibid.): market leading, subscription newspapers published in the large cities; national distribution, single-copy sales boulevard popular newspapers; niche, specialised or opinion newspapers catering to political, religious, sectoral, or financial audience segments; and low-circulation and low-frequency local newspapers catering to limited readerships. Denmark and Sweden also have free newspapers aiming at low-income and low-education readers (Schultz, 2007; Wadbring, 2007), a market segment that emerged in the 1990s that never took hold in Norway. Additionally, emerging since 2016–2017, is a segment of online-only hyperlocal news outlets sustained by a mix of subscription, advertising, and press support (Nygren et al., 2018; Høst, 2018). Present in these countries is also a handful of outspokenly right-wing media, although these must be considered fringe sites with peripheral roles in the news landscape. Overall, print circulation has declined since the 1990s, especially for tabloid newspapers. Nevertheless, print revenue still makes up the bulk of the income for most newspapers.

Media industries in Scandinavia share similarities in their ownership structures and cultures. Most newspapers started out as family-owned ventures, or were owned by local shareholders, organisations, or political parties. Income growth in the 1980s and 1990s, coupled with an increasing need for capital in the 2000s, led to a consolidation of companies, and some firms also went public. Newspaper ownership today is primarily private, with a mix of corporate, independent, and foundation ownership, and is predominantly national and regional in concentration, with some cross-border structures (Sjøvaag, 2019). Foundation ownership is on the rise in the region. The dominant ownership form in Sweden and Denmark, foundation ownership has spread to Norway, with the takeover of Amedia in 2016 by the foundation Sparebankstiftelsen DNB. Independent ownership occurs mostly at the local level (Sjøvaag & Pedersen, 2019), reflecting the dispersed character of Scandinavian newspaper markets (cf. Allern & Pollack, 2019). The relative strength of the Scandinavian local press structures is often attributed to the early introduction of press subsidies (Leckner et al., 2019), which has actively worked to sustain local newspapers, most of which would not survive without state support. Public ownership is another shared feature, most notably through public service broadcasting. Otherwise, ownership in the television sector is largely pan-Scandinavian, with Modern Times Group, Bonnier, and Egmont holding cross-border ownership of broadcasting structures. Media ownership in the region is thus generally characterised as highly concentrated (Ohlsson & Sjøvaag, 2019). Further concentration is in progress, with frequent ownership changes in recent years. In Sweden, for instance, one in two media houses have changed ownership since the turn of the millennium (Leckner et al., 2019). These consolidation processes coincide with the turn to AI, with scale becoming a dominant imperative for competitive advantage over differentiation strategies.

Ownership forms

Ownership refers to forms of governance and organisational influence (Schlosberg, 2016). As different ownership forms come with different kinds of expectations, media are subject to different kinds of powers, pressures, and controls. Owners exert two types of control over their media: allocation control and operational control. Allocation control allows owners to control the company's policy and strategy, its finances, resources, and profits, which enables mergers, acquisitions, and cut-backs. Operational control includes editorial strategies, deciding on leadership models, internal resource distribution, and hiring leaders and managers (McManus, 1994). For private media, this means the more shares that are owned by a single party, the more power it has over the company.

In the literature, ownership of media is either classified according to juridical corporate power structures (e.g., Picard & van Weezel, 2008), according to sectors (e.g., Benson, 2016; Hanitzsch & Berganza, 2012), or the level of profit orientation in the media (Humprecht & Esser, 2018). In its most basic form, ownership is dichotomised either as private or state ownership (e.g., Badr, 2021), or as publicly held (owned by shareholders) versus privately held (shareholder owned but not listed on the stock exchange) (Albarran, 2017). When ownership is described in terms of corporate structures, the question is what kind of ownership power can be wielded within the different ownership forms. Here, Picard and van Weezel (2008) distinguish between private, public, non-profit, and staff ownership. Each ownership form comes with its own set of corporate influence. When ownership is divided according to sectors, the focus is more on institutional logics (cf. Benson, 2016), and how different modes of power facilitate owners' influence on political processes (Benson et al., 2018). Here, Benson (2016) distinguishes between public, commercial, and civil society ownership. Benson et al. (2018) separate these logics according to stock market, privately held, civil society and public ownership and how these ownership forms shape the media's ability to perform public service. As we are concerned with the organisation of journalism and the markets for news in this context, Picard and van Weezel's (2008) classification presents the most suitable approach, as it is anchored in the various modes of corporate power that reside with their board structures and the different operational and allocative powers that various ownership forms allow.

Ownership thus matters because "all capital comes with conditions" (Ohlsson, 2012, p. 55). Public or state ownership comes with public oversight; stock market ownership entails quarterly reports and profit expectations; foundation ownership is thought to exercise more ideal forms of control (Graves & Konieczna, 2015) and lower profit expectations (Kaye & Quinn, 2010); while family ownership entails more limited control (cf. Sjøvaag & Ohlsson, 2019). The various powers that ownership forms allow also depend on the media system under which ownership is exercised.

State ownership of public service broadcasting is generally assumed to be benevolent in many European countries, while it is seen as potentially propagandistic in other systems such as in Asia, Africa, and Latin America. Hence, state control over public media is a question of how ownership influence is organised. State ownership can take several forms, including direct ownership (through public service broadcasting), through licensing or through financial means such as taxes or subsidies. In democratic corporatist states such as the Scandinavian ones, state power is limited through arm's length principles ensuring journalistic professionalism and editorial freedom (e.g., Syvertsen et al., 2014). In other political systems, such as in Spain and Greece, the ruling party has direct control over the public broadcaster (Hallin & Papathanassopoulos, 2002). In polarised pluralist media systems, industry is also thought to wield power over media (Hallin & Mancini, 2004).

Corporate ownership is either public (stock traded) or private. Publicly traded media companies tend to be large corporations focused on maximising shareholder value (Benson, 2016). Chain ownership refers to ownership of two or more outlets. The organisational traits of chains can have an effect on journalism, reflecting largely their corporate control mechanisms (Soloski, 1979). For instance, corporate management can extract profit from individual titles (Entman, 1989) to finance other parts of the operation. Chains can have a homogenising effect on news content as well as journalistic and editorial processes (Baker, 2006; Hendrickx, 2020). However, evidence is not conclusive concerning whether or not chains homogenise content (Berry & Waldfogel, 2001; Braun, 2015; Lacy, 1991; Sjøvaag, 2014a). Chains can nevertheless have an effect on the motivations of managers, as chains provide a corporate ladder that may incentivise workers to identify with the goals of the corporation over local affiliation. This effect also comes from the ability of the corporation to bring in managers that adhere to the corporate line (Parsons et al., 1988). In local communities, chains can also have a professionalising effect, creating more distance between newspapers and local sources of power, for instance from politicians and advertisers.

Family ownership occurs when a privately owned newspaper is handed down to a successor in the family. Many newspapers started out as family-owned enterprises, often turning into chains as companies expanded. As with foundation ownership, family-owned newspapers are thought to be able to withstand pressures from the markets because of the long-term strategies of the companies (Benson, 2016; Kaye & Quinn, 2010). Family-owned news enterprises face a couple of issues that makes them less sustainable in the long run though, including dilution of family power as control is handed down through generations, and access to capital from the markets. This has caused many family-owned newspapers to enter the stock market and become publicly traded.

Civil society ownership includes ownership by political parties, religious organisations, universities, and trade unions. The main form of civil society ownership today is foundation ownership, often referred to as trust ownership in the U.S. and U.K., but it also goes under the name non-profit or philanthropic ownership. This ownership form is on the rise in the U.S. as well as Scandinavia (Sjøvaag & Ohlsson, 2019; Nelson, 2018). Non-profit media tend to have strong public service ideals (Benson, 2018). In the U.S., non-profit news outlets largely seek funding from grants and donations rather than advertising revenue (Nelson, 2018). Hence, the profit expectation differs between the U.S. and Scandinavia. Scandinavian foundation-owned news typically relies on advertising revenue. Moreover, they are not exempt from profit expectations. Whereas U.S. trust ownership has been difficult to maintain, as it is beholden to donations (Ellis, 2011), Scandinavian foundations are formed to last for eternity. Another difference between the two ownership forms is that trusts are typically controlled by trustees who can dissolve the trust, whereas foundations are essentially ownerless (Ohlsson, 2012).

Scholars tend to see problems with all media ownership forms (Picard & Dal Zotto, 2016). This stands in opposition to how research tends to see ownership in other sectors – as a resource (Sjøvaag & Ohlsson, 2019). Most of the problems identified with media ownership forms have to do with influence, or the lack of influence, and the extent to which companies have social or profit goals. State ownership can be problematic because it prevents editors from pursuing political agendas. Large corporations are problematic because they can control content and markets. Corporate ownership is problematic because it tends to put profit ahead of social goals. Private owners can use their media to promote their personal interests, and small companies can come under pressure from powerful interests. Foreign ownership can affect national sovereignty. To that end, all ownership forms come with their own sets of strengths and weaknesses. However, as Picard and Dal Zotto (2016) have noted, "many of the complaints about ownership have nothing to do with ownership, but rather the commercialised nature of media and the pursuit of economic rewards" (p. 56). Moreover, ownership pressures on the media are generally thought to manifest indirectly (McChesney, 2003). To that end, ownership effects are difficult to operationalise.

Nevertheless, ownership influence is assumed along the entire value chain of news production, from journalistic practice to overall pluralism in society (cf. Hendrickx & Ranaivoson, 2021). Studies have found, for instance, that public service broadcasting adds to the diversity of political news in the media (Aalberg et al., 2010; Humprecht & Esser, 2018; Sjøvaag, Pedersen & Owren, 2019), and that foundation ownership fosters stronger public service values than other ownership forms (Benson, 2018). Studies have also found that competition can mitigate the homogenising effects of chain ownership (Baum & Zhukov, 2019; Sjøvaag & Pedersen, 2019). My own research from the Norwegian context has observed that ownership in itself has little effect on content diversity, largely due to the non-substitutability characteristics of local news. Instead, external pluralism has more to do with the presence of competition, niche orientation, and localism in the overall news landscape (Sjøvaag, Pedersen & Owren, 2019). Hence, the structural composition of Scandinavian media markets, particularly its dispersed nature, has a positive impact on media diversity. To that end, while ownership distribution clearly matters for external pluralism in media systems, structural differentiation plays an equally important part. In the Scandinavian context, this pertains in particular to the local structure of newspaper markets, often referred to as the 'backbone' of the media system in these countries (cf. Ekström et al., 2006; Mathisen, 2010).

Ownership consolidation in the region

Developments in ownership consolidation in Scandinavia have been traced from trade press reports from 2017–2022. The justification for this time-period is based on the scale advantages engendered by the rise of programmatic advertising, and 2017 was the year programmatic revenues took off across Scandinavian advertising markets (Ohlsson & Facht, 2017). Internationally, this timeframe also reflects when news companies began to link their futures to the digital (cf. Cawley, 2019). Trade press reports were analysed to gain insight into corporate explanations for, and industry reactions to, these consolidations (Corrigan, 2018). The databases of three trade publications were used, one in each country: *Mediawatch* in Denmark, *Medier24* in Norway and *Dagens Media* in Sweden.

Trends in ownership concentration in the Scandinavian newspaper industries all relate to business motivations. At the structural level, audience and advertising markets are in decline, digital uptake in the local press has been slow, and policy is largely reactive and incumbent-protective. On the market side, the main trends are local and niche consolidation, regional concentration, and cross-border collaboration. Seven tendencies are central to these trends:

1. Active consolidation strategies: Independently owned local newspapers are seeking ownership with their closest large competitor, often the market leader in the region.
2. Regional market concentration: Regional newspaper chains are buying up independent local and super-local newspapers in their geographical area, concentrating ownership in the regions.
3. Regional market consolidation: Large corporate chains are getting rid of minority shares in local newspapers adjacent to ongoing regional concentration processes.
4. Chain mergers: Local newspaper chains are merging with larger national chains.
5. Increasing cross-border ownership: Dominant newspaper chains in the three countries have ventured into acquisitions together.
6. Niche consolidation: Specialist publishers are buying other specialist publications, seeking like-minded partners to gain from scale advantages in digital affairs.

7. Niche competition: Dominant chains are buying niche media across media sectors (newspapers, magazines, podcasts) to differentiate their portfolios.

Structurally then, the markets are concentrating upward geographically, forming partnerships at all levels of publishing. As of yet, acquisition processes have only in a very few cases led new owners to merge titles operating in competition markets. Hence, while ownership concentration is taking place, there is little evidence of companies actively shutting down titles for revenue purposes. Let's look at these seven trends in a little more detail.

At the local level (1), independently owned newspapers are finding it hard to survive without the benefits of scale afforded by the infrastructures of larger corporate structures. In many cases, local newspapers actively seek corporate ownership, often from the regional market leader. Local acquisition processes are therefore often amicable affairs (cf. Sjøvaag et al., 2021). This concentrates markets at the regional level (2), where independent local papers and recently established online-only super-local newspapers are being bought by regional chains. This is exemplified by the regions of Trøndelag and Gudbrandsdalen in Norway. The regional newspaper chains Trønder-Avisa and Gudbrandsølen Dagningen have each acquired a number of independent local and super-local titles in their areas since 2017. Large national chains have retracted from regions where mergers are happening (3), creating new opportunities for market control by these regional chains. Hence, chains are moving their resources away from minority shares in consolidating markets, and they are selling titles in markets where this constitutes competition in local/regional advertising markets. For instance, the Danish foundation-owned media company JP/Politikens Hus has sold the Swedish local newspaper chain Lokaltidningen, allowing the Swedish media company Bonnier to gain a stronger presence in the south of the country, increasing ownership concentration at the national level. Patching up holes in these geographic markets has thus led to both sales and acquisitions, fostering price control within local, regional, and national markets, and creating local/regional efficiencies in the distribution of journalistic labour resources.

As for chain mergers, national corporations have bought local newspaper chains across the region (4), exemplified by the acquisition of Nordsjø Media by Amedia in Norway (2019), and the Polaris acquisition of Agderposten Medier in the same country (2020). In Sweden, Gota Media was bought by NMT in 2018, Ortstidnigar i Väst was sold to Stampen in 2019, and Tidningar i Norr was sold to VK Media in 2021. In all these cases, mid-sized chains with 4–13 papers have merged with larger, national chains. These are, again, relatively amicable processes where local newspapers have welcomed their inclusion into larger corporate structures. Mergers are thus framed as necessary from the point of view of the acquired entity, and as a market opportunity for the acquiring firm.

At the Scandinavian level, partnerships are forming across nationally dominant newspaper chains (5), particularly across the Norway-Sweden border, where Bonnier has formed partnerships with Amedia, and Polaris has partnered with NWT to buy Swedish local newspaper chains. National chains that seek to expand their holdings are to some extent limited from doing so in their national markets because of ownership concentration rules. Seeking assets across borders is generally welcomed rather than being viewed with suspicion. This can largely be attributed to shared cultures of editorial and professional ideals, common structural media welfare state conditions, and regional affinity for guarding against 'foreign' interests. It is thus seen as preferable to stay within the 'Scandinavian family' rather than come under the ownership of media companies based in less welfare state-oriented countries (see Sjøvaag & Owren, 2021b).

While there are certainly differences in organisational properties and cultures across the three countries, the similarities outweigh the differences to the extent that Scandinavian mergers are a lot less culturally fraught than, say, acquisitions by corporations based in the U.K. (a liberal media system) or Poland (a polarised pluralist system). Worth mentioning here is also the fact that major stakeholders in the media sectors in all three countries know each other and have a history of cooperation, not only through cross-border ownership (e.g., in the publishing and television sectors), but also on policy issues in terms of protecting and advancing the media welfare state in relation to the European Union. Because of language similarities, media industries' operatives in the three countries can also easily follow developments in the other markets through the trade press. In addition, several agencies work actively to foster collaboration across the region, for instance through the Nordic Council of Ministers.

Aiming to gain from the same type of scale advantages, specialist publishers have begun seeking niche publications (6). Niche media are buying other niche media to consolidate operating costs to attain scale advantages. In Norway, for instance, NHST, the owner of the leading financial paper *Dagens Næringsliv*, has recently invested in the cultural and agricultural presses, expanding their niche markets. Moreover, newspaper companies are investing in niche media from across the media landscape (7). Examples here include JP/Politikens Hus buying medical and design publications, and Schibsted sweeping the Norwegian podcast market. Some of these ventures are efforts to expand business-to-business markets while others aim to secure emerging markets and attain critical mass to enable subscription paywalls, such as in the case of the podcast market in Norway.

All these mergers and acquisitions processes have accelerated since 2017. In most cases, business decisions and corporate strategies are guided by some notion of 'fit'. The market is concentrating, and everyone is looking around to ensure they end up with the best ownership fit for their organisation. Local newspapers and smaller chains prefer foundation ownership to stock traded ownership, and they prefer to merge with structures that share some geographic affiliation and cultural like-mindedness.

Structurally, changes are also happening in the forms of ownership:

1. Foundation ownership is on the rise.
2. Family ownership is decreasing further as family-owned enterprises are sold to corporations.

Foundations have been the most active buyers in the market in recent years, in large part due to local papers' higher willingness-to-be-bought by foundations over publicly traded companies. The difference between private and foundation ownership can thus be seen as a driver of consolidation processes. Foundations increasingly present as attractive corporate structures to merge with. Whereas commercial ownership is regarded as a profit-run enterprise where risks are tied to cut-backs and lay-offs to secure shareholder profits during economic downturns, foundations typically have either a charitable or ideological cause (Ohlsson, 2012). Foundation ownership does not, however, relieve newspapers from operating according to for-profit principles. Family ownership is, moreover, becoming increasingly difficult to sustain, leading many families to sell their newspapers, exemplified by the sale of Lindköpings Tidningen to NWT, and the sale of Hall Media to Amedia (49 percent) and MittMedia (51 percent), in Sweden over the past couple of years.

Cost is the main driver of these structural consolidations. Digital synergies drive willingness-to-buy as well as willingness-to-be-bought. In order to drive down cost per unit, companies need to either scale up or down. And while some companies have chosen to adjust costs to a sustainable level by scaling down, fixed technology costs, and the cost of constant development on both the advertising and audience sides of the market, drive most companies to scale up. For some companies increased scale has meant additional resources as local newspapers are included in large, digital operations. In other cases, cost adjustment to conform to lower advertising income and slow digital innovation has resulted in staff reductions in local papers joining larger chains. Seeking new revenue, many companies venture into new areas of operation, such as business-to-business, business services, and social media – strategies that also require additional resources. Seeking scale advantages on the technology side of the industry thus leads to concentration across the board, from the local to the Scandinavian level.

Based on this analysis, the following enduring market characteristics of news can be identified:

1. Scale advantages continue to be an important driver: Buying and selling to patch up market dominance, either getting rid of loose affiliations in markets with low penetration or buying up independents or chains to fortify geographic markets on a regional level.
2. Price control in advertising markets: News corporations continue to strive for umbrella market effects, controlling local newspapers in an area in combination with the regional market leader engenders price control in regional advertising markets.
3. High fixed costs and low variable costs: Increased efficiency through synergy drives willingness-to-be-bought as well as willingness-to-buy, lowering cost per unit. Fixed costs in the form of technology investments, corporate monitoring and publishing can be driven down if spread among multiple entities.
4. The two-sided market model remains in effect: News organisations adjust their price structures to accommodate changes in their dual markets. More cost reverts to the audience side through increased subscription prices as well as digital paywalls. Corporations seek additional revenue through business-to-business enterprise.

Market failure

The regulation of media ownership in Scandinavia is designated to the general competition authority, and there is no special provision for newspaper markets. Regulators in Denmark, Sweden, and Norway are all aware of the concentration happening in the newspaper structure, and policy documents point to the economic and technological realities behind this shift (NOU, 2017, p. 7; SKLS, 2018; SOU, 2016). It is difficult for policy to establish instruments to mitigate such concentration tendencies, but incentives are in place to support independent local media financially in the digital transition. In most cases, however, infrastructural upgrades are beyond the scope of what small, local newsrooms can handle on their own, even if they are part of a regional chain operation. The space between market realities and state intervention where newspapers sit (cf. Murdock & Golding, 2005) thus grows increasingly contested, as policy is also limited from overly regulating the structure of private ownership based on freedom of speech principles (c.f. Sjøvaag, 2019). News media in Scandinavia operate in mixed markets consisting of private media ownership alongside state owned public service broadcasting (Allern & Blach-Ørsten, 2011), where state intervention is governed by arm's length principles. There is thus a limit to how much intervention states can impose without infringing the free speech principles that support private ownership in the sector. To that end, fear of market failure is a cornerstone of Scandinavian media regulations (Sjøvaag, 2014b), aimed at ensuring external pluralism (Hallin & Mancini, 2004) at the media systems level.

The concept of market failure is not much used in journalism research (Pickard, 2019). Nor is it employed all that often in media industries studies. The question of market failure does, however, arise quite frequently in the context of public service media (e.g., Berg et al., 2013; Cunningham & Flew, 2015; Helm, 2005), and has therefore been more readily applied within the political economy strand of communication research. It was on the agenda, for instance, during the digitalisation of broadcasting spectrums around 2010, when the question of spectrum scarcity arose and challenged the need for government intervention in media markets. Market failure has also been used to promote state regulation of telecommunications sectors and securing universal services (Garnham, 1997). This principle is thus well established in democratic corporatist media systems, where market failure serves as the primary justification for government intervention in media markets, most notably through public service broadcasting and press support (Lund, 2007; NOU, 2017, p. 7). While media welfare states justify intervention to sustain pluralism, within liberal media systems such as the U.K., government support to media is justified mainly as a measure to sustain competition and market equilibrium (Curran & Seaton, 2003). To that end, what counts as market failure depends on a society's ambition for its media system (Berg et al., 2013).

Market failure as a concept is derived from neoclassical economic theory and refers to the inability of the market to effectively allocate important goods and services (Pickard, 2017). Market failure thus explains "a circumstance where the pursuit of private interest does not lead to an efficient use of society's resources or a fair distribution of society's goods" (Vining & Weimer, 1992 p. 13, cited in Zerbe Jr. & McCurdy, 1999). It is based on the premise that some goods and services have high social value but low commercial viability, and are thus less likely to be universally available if provided on a purely commercial basis. It explains when governments may need to intervene in markets that display inefficiency when left to their own devices (Murschetz, 2020). Not all products will be profitable for commercial enterprises to produce with optimal quality. For some products, then, the market alone cannot meet the social, political, or cultural needs for such products.

Market failure is thus closely related to other economic concepts such as externalities and merit goods (Cunningham & Flew, 2015). Merit goods, or public goods, are goods that society needs but that individuals tend to undervalue. Examples frequently used include museums, health care, education, and clean air. Hence, the full cost of the product goes beyond the transaction itself, causing externalities as well as possible free-riding issues (Berg et al., 2013). Neoclassical political economists tend to agree that government intervention should be minimised and reserved for such merit goods (Winseck, 2012). Hence, market failure is strongly associated with media policy and regulation, largely used to legitimate public intervention deemed necessary to avoid potential societal and economic losses. Helm (2005), however, also points out that market failures are often multiple and relative, and are thus rarely straightforward, requiring a multitude of policy instruments. This makes corrective policy difficult, risky, and prone to failure on its own terms (Murschetz, 2020; Pickard, 2013). Scholars are, moreover, divided on how effective the market is in regulating competition (Winseck, 2012). They also disagree on exactly how effective governments can be in regulating markets (Zerbe Jr. & McCurdy, 1999). In essence, then, market failure is a normative argument that contains a critical reaction to free market assumptions (Berg et al., 2013). Murschetz (2020) therefore argues that market failure is unhelpful in terms of grasping journalism's crisis, because the theory is premised on neoclassical economic assumptions, including the possibility of perfect competition.

Profit maximisation is nevertheless at the root of the market failure thesis (Pickard, 2014) – the assumption that market driven media will under produce content that is critical to deliberation (Horwitz, 2005). Market failure in media industries can occur when investments are withheld because expenditures cannot extract the necessary returns, or when customers fail to pay for the full social benefit of such services (Pickard, 2017, p. 65), which in journalism's case refers to audiences and advertisers. Market concentration can be part of such market failures, as can profit maximisation – situations that could prompt government intervention to ensure distribution of power in media ownership conducive to democratic pluralism. Over the last decade, Pickard (2013; 2015) has mobilised market failure arguments when promoting government intervention in U.S. news markets. To Pickard (2015), the U.S. market systematically under-produces journalism, qualifying as a case for market failure. Pickard (2013) says journalism is affected by two kinds of market failure, namely insufficient support for positive externalities and failure to hinder monopolistic concentration that leads to abuses of market power and the degradation of quality journalism. Market failure in journalism's case thus amounts to ensuring that news industries are able to provide the information that citizens need to sustain democracy, to enable news to reach these citizens, and to prevent concentration to hinder the spread of a diversity of views and contents to audiences.

Perhaps what we are looking at here are three kinds of market failure, or rather – two counts of market failure and one count of policy failure. On the one hand, the business side failure of not providing enough quality journalism, caused by the concentration of ownership power and profit motives. On the other hand, failure on the part of the market in not securing enough income from advertising and paying audiences to make news profitable, caused in large part by the proliferation of social media. The policy failure in this regard amounts to the inability of regulators to mobilise policy tools that are adaptable enough to ensure quality journalism undergoing rapid change, while at the same time ensuring that policy instruments do not hinder competition or innovation. Policy tends to protect incumbents in the news industries, not least because incumbents also have the insight, networks, and resources to lobby governments effectively. Policy also does not have the jurisdiction to regulate the platform players effectively. To date, they have been able to ensure neither the transparency, privacy, nor data ethics called for by industry, academic, and media monitoring agencies (although the European Union Digital Services Act certainly attempts this). Nor have they been able to impose so-called Google-tax on platform companies that operate within their jurisdiction, ensuring that welfare is returned to the markets in which they profit. While market failure principles are clearly relevant to the operations of tech giants in regional markets, they are in essence difficult to operationalise in its current scope, in which national companies play by national rules in a media ecosystem that is global in scale and driven by principles developed in the context of the digital markets in the U.S.

Chain consolidation as a solution

Being one of the main drivers behind market failure concerns, ownership consolidation in the Scandinavian newspaper industries indicates that power will continue to concentrate in this sector. This is particularly concerning at the local level, where independent newspaper ownership has been a cornerstone of the media/political system in the three countries (Sjøvaag, 2019), especially as it relates to representation, centre-periphery conflicts, and civic engagement. Ownership concentration, and in particular monopoly situations, disrupts the distribution of communicative power (Baker, 2006), which can lead to a decrease in opinion pluralism and content diversity in the public sphere. Chain ownership can have a homogenising effect in this regard, consolidating content across markets. Recent research (Sjøvaag & Pedersen, 2019) suggests, however, that chain ownership may have a limited effect on this kind of homogenisation, especially if that ownership is concentrated on local newspapers operating in monopolistic markets. Due to the nature of local news, being non-substitutable and thus difficult to synergise or centralise, the owners of a chain of local newspapers are limited in the amount of content overlap they can engage with. There are, however, synergy effects in these arrangements, due in large part to the increased needs posed by digitalisation, algorithmic curation, and programmatic advertising that requires larger sets of data, corporate-wide content management systems, and analytical expertise. Hence, while owners may not use their power to push editorial decisions or even content priorities in certain directions, chain ownership nevertheless affords scale advantages conducive to economic rewards (cf. Picard & Dal Zotto, 2016), including resource distribution, technological and organisational measures, and the hiring of leaders and managers (McManus, 1994).

In these regional news markets, then, chain consolidation and ownership concentration present as a solution to the growing competition from the technology sector, in particular in search and social media. Ownership concentration also presents as a solution to avoid market failure in individual local communities, as scaling up prevents local press structures from going under. A cultural component is clearly present in these processes, both at the level of industry and at the level of the media welfare state. All these mergers and acquisitions are driven by a concern for ‘fit’, based in some notion of like-mindedness, the results of which are rather conflict-free consolidations welcomed by all parties. A weakness in this analysis, however, stems from the source material itself – trade press magazines that are generally more tuned into industry and management issues rather than the effect of these processes on journalism itself. Overall, the trade magazines themselves as well as the news managers, CEOs, and politicians they interview are promoting the same crisis narrative that can also be found in the research literature – one in which journalism faces dire economic challenges because of the impact of platform players on the two-sided market model, the solutions to which are organisational, technological, and managerial.

In the next chapter, I examine in further detail how the economy of the news industries is dealt with in two different and often contradictory theoretical frameworks – in media economics and management literature, and in the tradition of the political economy of communication. These perspectives will furthermore be evaluated in the context of a more institutional approach, namely the new economic sociology.

4 Theoretical perspectives

Media scholars have always been in the business of (a) criticising the media for failing to live up to their potential and (b) suggesting solutions to remedy these failures. The critical political economic tradition tends to blame capitalism (and the profit motive) for journalism's shortcomings; strategic management tends to blame managers. The two traditions recognise slightly different problems. Critical scholars tend to single out commercialisation, tabloidisation, and bias as the failures of journalism, while management scholars tend to focus on inertia, or the inability of media organisations to adapt to change. Both traditions have been concerned with the survival of the press as an industry when facing digital disruption and loss of income and readership. The solutions the two traditions propose display stark differences between them. Critical political economy tends to turn to regulation and public funding, and thus the state, for solutions. Strategic management tends to suggest innovation in product, production, and management. Critical political economy thus recognises the problems of journalism as internal (greedy owners), and the solution as external (state intervention). Strategic management often sees the problem as external (new competitors), and the solution as internal (adapt or die).

When journalism is approached as an industry, it is either studied through a sociological lens, or through the lens of media economics and management. The sociological direction is rooted in the social sciences, while the other is born out of business schools. The roots of the two traditions are thus political economy and neoclassical economics. As journalism studies is born out of vocational training schools (Kleis Nielsen, 2016), the academic foundation of journalism research is largely tied to theories of professionalism and production – so, to sociology and political economy. Media industries research is based in the cultural studies tradition on questions of labour, content, and production, as well as management research with roots in economics. While scholarship today is indeed more agnostic than this dichotomisation suggests, these paradigms do

DOI: 10.4324/9781003081791-4

provide the basic frameworks for scientific explanations of how the media work in society. It is thus worthwhile to trace their origins in the context of journalism's digital disruptions, not least in defining problems and seeking solutions.

Before outlining the basics of each tradition and their various theoretical offspring, it is worth noting a few fundamental differences between media management and critical political economy and how they view the media. The intellectual forefather of media management studies is Adam Smith, the author of *The Wealth of Nations* (1776) often credited with establishing the free market mantra. Critical political economy takes its understanding of economy and society from Karl Marx and his historical materialist view of power. Critical political economy thus takes class and social relations as its methodological starting point, while media management is based in methodological individualism, where individual motivations and actions are seen to shape social phenomena. Critical political economy scholars tend to study markets as national entities, largely because economics is tied to policy and regulation, and thus national jurisdiction. Media management has a more holistic definition of markets, as they are tied to concepts of competition and thus product markets. Research in critical political economy tends to segment media markets according to their technologies (broadcasting, newspaper, internet), while media management tends to consider markets according to content type or labour. The traditions also have a few important commonalities. They agree, for instance, that there are fundamental problems with the assumptions of neoclassical economics, particularly the idea that individuals are rational and that markets can be perfectly competitive. They also agree on the value of public goods, and they are equally concerned about market failure.

The two traditions under investigation here thus have opposing views on what shapes action and change in society. Political economy considers structure, and in particular how economic and political power is distributed in society, as determinants of the social order. Media management and economics considers agency as primary. The agency/structure (cf. Giddens, 1984) dichotomy with which media markets are typically approached thus almost completely overlooks the role of institutions. To account for this oversight, once these two dominant perspectives have been introduced and discussed, I will present a third option that considers how economic action is embedded in social reality (Swedberg, 2006). The framework of new economic sociology will be mobilised here to demonstrate how economic behaviour can be seen as part of institutional behaviour, bridging the agency/structure dichotomy. This perspective helps to explain how the business of journalism is shaped by the logic of the institution, and how economic action within the news industries amounts to path-dependent and core-protecting behaviour that shields the enduring forms of journalism during digital disruption.

The roots: sociology and economy

We begin this theoretical review by tracing the origins of media industries studies to its two roots – sociology and economy. An industry is as much about business and competition as it is about the production of goods and their role in society. In media industries research, production and labour research tends to take a critical approach, and is thus rooted in Marxism, while the study of business and management tends to be non-critical and is rooted in economics. In the sociological perspective, the distribution of resources in society is the result of political struggle. What resources you end up with depends on your position in relation to labour and production. Thus, class is important. Capitalism here amounts to a social relation between workers and the owners of the means of production. Profit in this system is generated from the exploitation of labour (Garnham 1995; 2007). In classical economics, competition is seen as the cornerstone of capitalism (Flew, 2012) – a market system based on private property (Mosco, 2008). To Adam Smith, competition was a solution to the unfair distribution of capital to the already wealth class of property owners. The question here was how to allocate resources that satisfied certain needs over others (Hardy, 2014a; Wasko, 2005). Sociology (class) and economy (capitalism) thus come together as *political economy* – the relationship between political and economic interest (or state and capital) in organising labour, controlling resources, and distributing value (Miller, 2014).

Political economy is the study of the relationship between the market and the state, and how the two forces influence individuals, groups, and society at large. Therefore, political economy pertains to questions of production and trade, the distribution of wealth, and the governance of relations, including the role of laws, cultures, and norms. Political economy involves issues of influence and process, including how political and economic forces affect resource distribution, and how the relations that shape relationships sustain and transform them over time. In media scholarship, political economy reflects key issues in the relationship between capitalism and democracy (McChesney, 2013), and is thus about power relations, class systems, and structural inequalities (Flew, 2012), often critical of the status quo (Gandy, 1992). Mosco's definition (2009) is often mobilised in the literature, where "political economy is the study of the social relations, particularly the power relations, that mutually constitute the production, distribution, and consumption of resources, including communication resources" (p. 2). While it is common to trace political economy to Marx' historical materialism (e.g., Pereira, 2009), its roots are also attributed to the historical sociology of Adam Smith (Garnham, 2014). To that end, political economy is a mix of Marxian and economic perspectives (Mosco, 2009).

Political economy as applied to media is about the relationship between communication, democracy, and capitalism. McChesney (2000, p. 110) defines the political economy of communication as the study of the nature of the relationship between media and communication systems and the broader social structure of society, and how it influences existing class and social relations. It considers structural factors in evaluating how media and communication systems affect political and social power and to what extent they serve as forces for or against democracy and self-government (McChesney, 2013, p. 64). For that reason, scholarship tends to focus on the problems associated with dominant commercial media. This is also one of the aspects of the political economy of communication that frequently receives criticism – its predominant focus on the power of monopoly capital without considering the complexity and uncertainty of media markets and industries (Winseck, 2011).

Political economy perspectives began to influence media studies in the 1960s over exactly these types of questions – a growing concern for the impact of private ownership in cultural production (Fenton, 2007). To that end, the political economy of the media is really a *critical* political economy of the media, highly influenced by Marxism (Hardy, 2014a). Whereas the political economy of communications has been accused of taking money for granted and for seeing the economic as separate from the political (Graham, 2006), critical political economy does not consider economics as a separate domain but considers the interplay between economic organisation and political, social, and cultural life. Murdock & Golding (2005) say it considers "how the organisation of media industries impinges on the production and circulation of meaning and the ways in which people's options for consumption and use are structured by their position within the general economic formation" (p. 61). The critical political economy of the media is thus concerned with corporate power, ownership concentration and control, and how the market impacts on the role of media in public communication. Critical political economy perspectives on communication focus on the production of cultural goods, issues of representation (in text) and material, and cultural inequality (caused by or reflected in consumption) and thus tend to promote social change, social justice, emancipation, resistance, and intervention (Dahlberg, 2011; Hardy, 2014b; Murdock & Golding, 2005; Wasko, 2014). To that end, a critical political economy of communication is really about "power in communications and the conditions for realizing democracy" (Hardy, 2014b, p. 190).

The 'critical' in critical political economy is essentially a Marxist critique of power. As Wasko (2014) explains, though, due to the history of persecution of the intellectual left in the United States, 'critical' in this respect serves as a euphemism (see also Cunningham et al., 2015). The way these theoretical traditions are described by the scholars involved makes it seem like political economy and critical political economy are the same thing – concerned with class, power, and justice. There are, however, directions in political economy that are not as 'critical', in the sense that research here rests less overtly on Marxism. The new economic sociology, for instance, takes inspiration also from the works of Max Weber and Emile Durkheim, and thus mobilises institutional perspectives into political economy. As Swedberg (2006) explains, economic sociology is the application of sociology to economic phenomena, whereas political economy applies the logics of economics to political phenomena. Economic sociology puts economic processes in their social context, investigating how material conditions are influenced by social processes (Fligstein, 2015). Like most political economic frameworks, economic sociology rejects many of the principles in neoclassical and microeconomic theory. Rather than thinking of actors as rationally maximising their own interest, they consider actors as social agents and economic action as social action. They also see the economy as part of the social system rather than separate from it. Scholars in this tradition (e.g., Dimaggio & Powell, 1991; Fligstein, 1990; Granovetter, 1985; Sen, 1986; Swedberg et al., 1987) argue that rationality is socially determined, that institutions work as rationality contexts, and that economic actions are interest struggles influenced by power. New economic sociology has, however, rarely been applied to media markets (Will & Gossel, 2017). Instead, the question of media, markets and politics continued to be dominated by critical political economy perspectives until more culturalist approaches emerged during the expansion of media studies in the 1980s (Hardy, 2014b).

Cultural studies emerged from the Frankfurt School and focuses on consumption and reception over questions of work and production (Garnham, 1995). The Frankfurt School refers to a group of German scholars who developed critical theory by applying Marxist analysis on the conditions for social relations within capitalist systems. Key figures in this tradition who were influential in cultural studies include Adorno and Horkheimer (1997) and their analysis of the standardisation of cultural production. Cultural studies is thus more about popular cultural practices and social agency than it is about elite practices and structural factors (Fenton, 2007; McChesney, 2000). From cultural studies came the cultural industries school which focuses on how media make and circulate texts that influence how we see the world (Hesmondhalgh, 2013). Central works include Bernard Miège's

(1989) analysis of the development of culture within capitalism, and Raymond Williams' (1983) work on culture and society. Cultural industries scholars address questions of contradiction, symbolic creation, the social relations of cultural production, and tensions between production and consumption. Critical approaches to the cultural industries tend to focus on the impact of capitalism on workers' autonomy and the diversity of content in the media, while non-critical approaches include more functional analyses of how industries are organised to bring products to market (Havens, 2014). Media industries studies are often positioned as a subset within the cultural industries school (ibid.), but media industries studies also involve research practices from business research and organisational sociology. Kellner (2009) thus argues that media industries studies manage to bridge the divide between political economic studies of media and communication and the cultural studies tradition. To understand why this assertion is important, we first need to understand what this divide is about.

There have been enduring tensions between cultural studies and the critical political economy of communications across many decades (Hardy, 2014b). The most volatile clashes between the two traditions took place in the 1970s through to the 1990s. Often referred to as the 'blindspot debate', it was initiated by Dallas Smythe in 1977 and concerned the question of the audience commodity. Smythe argued that the media's main product is the audience, sold by media to advertisers. Smythe here essentially called for a return of economics to the centre of Marxist investigations of the media, which Graham Murdock (1978), in response to Smythe, argued revealed a blindspot concerning the role of the state and the independent role of media in producing dominant ideologies. Smythe (1977) said that media fulfilled four important purposes through the audience commodity: creating consumerism, confirming the ideology of monopoly capitalism, producing supportive public opinion, and gaining economic importance through profitability. Murdock claimed, however, that making revenue from audiences was different from making revenue from advertisers. Murdock here essentially argued for a separation of industries in analysis, and for seeing media artefacts as operating on two levels, both economic and cultural (cf. Meehan, 2002).

This initial debate reveals a longstanding contradiction between the European tradition and the American approach to communications studies. While both traditions rest on neo-Marxist thought, European scholars were anchored in cultural studies and the cultural industries approach (Miege, 1989), whereas American scholars rested on what Hesmondhalgh (2002) has called the Schiller-McChesney tradition, which also includes institutional perspectives (Wasko, 2005), and a critique of monopoly capitalism. The nomenclature that Hesmondhalgh mobilises refers to two central scholars in the field, Herbert Schiller and Robert McChesney, who focused on the role of capitalist economy in citizenship and democracy (e.g., Herman & McChesney, 1997; Schiller, 1969). The debate between cultural studies and political economy reflects another longstanding dispute within the social sciences across the Atlantic, namely the question of what role the critical perspective should really have in scholarship. This is referred to as the administrative/critical debate, taking place in the 1940s, where 'administrative' research, or research commissioned by industry, was criticised for not containing a critical dimension (cf. Winseck, 2017).

To that end, political economic approaches to communication are often associated with left-wing theory. This has inspired many scholars to engage in passionate exercises of demarcation, particularly regarding the interpretation and mobilisation of Marx in communication scholarship. Garnham (1995) has stated that he wanted to "rescue the concept [of political economy] from […] the immense and damaging condescension of cultural studies" (p. 63). He characterises (2014) cultural studies' portrayal of political economy as "a vague, crude, and unself-questioning form of Marxism, linked to a gestural and self-satisfied, if often paranoid, radicalism" (p. 42), with a romantic Marxist rejection of the market. In these debates, then, each side tends to oversimplify the characteristics (and flaws) of the other side, with ensuing rounds of posturing from the opposition (Meehan, 1999). Both traditions claim to be the most holistic and comprehensive, while the other is neglectful of crucial features. Tensions also arise when scholars attempt to identify what the differences between the two approaches really amount to. In essence, the debate is about economy versus culture (McChesney, 1997). Political economists analyse production while cultural studies investigate consumption. Political economy looks at the social totality while cultural studies renounces this level of analysis as impossible. Mosco (2009) has said that the two directions depart on the issue of subjectivity, accusing cultural studies of exaggerating its importance. On the other hand, cultural studies have accused political economy research of neglecting the role of agency (Cunningham et al., 2015), overlooking cultural practices and the importance of symbolic form (Mansell, 2004), and of underestimating the context of interaction (Pereira, 2009). The main difference, then, says Fenton (2007), boils down to an opposition between economic reductionism versus cultural specificity.

The Marxist hue with which political economy is painted in these debates had led many scholars to refrain from identifying with the tradition (Winseck, 2017). In fact, the stereotypical tone of these "ritualised" (Meehan, 1999, p. 150), "irreconcilable" (Fenton, 2007, p. 8) and "spiteful" (Wasko, 2005, p. 43) debates has caused many new approaches to reject political economy as a viable framework for media analysis (Wasko, 2018).

Scholars have begun calling for an integration of the two approaches in the 2000s (Fenton, 2007; Hardy, 2014b; Wasko, 2005). Cunningham and colleagues (2015) have thus observed that "the passion once associated with this debate has died down somewhat" (p. 52), partly due to the rise of new perspectives. But tensions still prevail. The debate resurfaced when Paul Dwyer argued in 2015 that political economy approaches to the media have failed to contribute to the understanding of the changing organisation of media as systems of meaning-making. Murdock and Golding (2016) were quick to respond, claiming the author had misunderstood political economy. Overall, however, the critical political economy of communications has experienced some displacement in media industries research with the emergence of new directions and objects of study, including media systems, convergence, institutional theory, and policy research. There has been a shift towards more integrated perspectives and theoretical complexity. However, the analysis of digital labour has made Marx relevant again (Hardy, 2014b), particularly through the focus on work, intellectual property, and precarity (Holt & Perren, 2019; Miller, 2014).

Media industries studies are part of this new diversification of research perspectives that actively tries to move beyond the dichotomy of cultural studies versus political economy (Holt & Perren, 2019). Definitions of media industries studies tend to be rather fuzzy, but research here tends to concern the structure of markets, patterns of ownership, strategies of key players, and trajectory of developments (Winseck, 2012). It concerns the political, cultural, and economic dimensions of media as industries and their role in the production and circulation of culture (Herbert et al., 2020). Humanities-based scholars in this field have moved into questions of creative labour, platforms and algorithmic culture, infrastructures and data studies, digital media and materiality, privacy and surveillance studies, and they also consider environmental issues. Hence, humanistic approaches to media industries have roots in critical theory. Scholars from the sociological tradition also mobilise political economy perspectives into this field, including non-critical versions of political economy, for instance through infrastructure studies (cf. Flensburg & Lai, 2020), and through studies of the information economy.

In this emerging research field, some leading figures seem intent to already label efforts along the cultural studies–political economy divide (e.g., Havens et al., 2009; Holt & Perren, 2019). While such stock-taking has its merits, attempts at carrying the 'blindspot' debate through to this rather synthesising field that as-of-yet allows for rather diverse theoretical approaches to media industry phenomena, seems to me to be moot at best and counter-productive at worst; not least because media industries studies not only contains culturalist and institutional approaches, but also economic and business studies approaches. Understanding media in the context of digital disruption requires an understanding also of the digital economy, digital markets, and the data logics that govern them. From a journalism studies perspective, economic dimensions of news production only came into view when the business model started to fail. The role of platforms, and the economic principles of the digital economy, have thus gained relevance as scholars attempt to make sense of what is happening to journalism (e.g., Nielsen 2016; Peters, 2019). This is a welcome expansion of the theoretical context in which journalism is understood. Media industries studies consider industries to have cultural as well as economic and institutional dimensions. Politics as well as economics influence the trajectory with which the economic sustainability of journalism can be achieved. At the same time, a growing focus on journalism's sustainability as practice and profession has found inspiration in organisational and management studies largely born out of business schools.

The other approach: economics

Neoclassical economics is the dominant version of economics that emerged in the 1870s and whose assumptions continue to carry through to scholarship today. As such, it remains the 'great other' to which social scientists as well as media business scholars devote vast amounts of effort refuting. Neoclassical economics is the study of how producers meet the needs of consumers through buying and selling goods in the context of scarce resources (Flew, 2012). Neoclassical economics proposes that this process is regulated by a number of constant assumptions, namely that of utility, perfect information, rational actors, and costless transactions (Cunningham et al., 2015; Menard & Shirley, 2005). Here, consumers are considered to be rational, utility maximising agents who can have access to perfect information about the products on offer in a market and make purchasing decision based on those premises, and to do so first and foremost to promote their own welfare. These assumptions are problematic because consumption is not always rational and because competition does not necessarily lead to a maximisation of wellbeing (Hesmondhalgh, 2013). There is general agreement about the problematic aspects of these assumptions across the theoretical board discussed in relation to the media industries, also in media economics.

Media economics is the application of conventional neoclassical microeconomic theory to the media industries (Picard, 2006). Media economics is the study of "how media industries use scarce resources to produce content that is distributed among consumers in a society to satisfy various wants and needs" (Albarran 2010, p. 3), or "how media operators meet the information and entertainment wants and needs of audiences, advertisers and society with available resources" (Picard 1989, p. 5). It has neoclassical foundations in the sense that competition is seen as the driving force creating a system of relative prices and resource allocation (Flew, 2012). While Wasko (2005) has accused media economics of celebrating capitalism, media economics is also critical of neoclassical assumptions that actors are rational and utility maximising and the conditions of perfect and imperfect competition (Hardy, 2014a).

The application of microeconomic theory means that media economics is mainly oriented towards individual firms, industries, and markets. According to Picard (2006) media economics consists of three traditions, including a theoretical tradition (applying concepts from neoclassical economics), an applied tradition (studying the structure of industry and their markets) and a critical tradition (welfare economic perspectives influenced by cultural studies). Picard notes that the theoretical and applied approaches are often combined, and that the critical tradition stands somewhat apart from the other two. The critical tradition is here identified as influenced by political economy and cultural studies, for which Picard designates the central figures in critical political economy – Janet Wasko, Vincent Mosco, and Nicholas Garnham. Whereas the critical approach has focused on concentration and monopoly, labour and work issues, theoretical and applied approaches have been more concerned with how to achieve competitive advantage in the industry and how to cope with structural changes.

The co-presence of critical political economy perspectives alongside microeconomic theory in the field has not been without its tensions, as Picard (ibid.) notes. His view of this conflict is that it is unnecessary and counter-productive, as each contributes important evidence in their own right. Picard has observed, in general, that the economics of the media have largely been ignored by media scholars. This is not only due to the fact that few media scholars come from economics, or that few academic media programmes contain media economics course elements. Picard also asserts that media executives themselves never used to consider media to be business enterprises. The field has, however, grown in relevance because business principles and market dynamics are increasingly important to understand the challenges and transformations of the media in digital disruption (Hardy, 2014a).

The dominant theoretical framework applied in media economics is the Industrial Organisation (IO) framework, including questions of strategy and firm behaviour. The Industrial Organisation model "allows the analysis of a particular industry or market by examining the market structure. This structure affects firm conduct, which in turn affects firm performance" (Lacy & Noh, 1997, p. 8). This is referred to as the Structure-Conduct-Performance model (SCP) (Porter, 1985), used to understand how the number of firms in a market, their products and the entry barriers shape conduct and performance variables in an industry (Baumann, 2020; Mierzejewska, 2011). The paradigm is based on the question of how much control a firm can have, which grows with market concentration. In the Industrial Organisation model, there are only two basic competitive advantages, namely low cost or cost advantages, and differentiation (Porter, 1985, p. 119).

Central to analysis within this framework is Porter's 'five forces' (Porter, 1980) outlining the forces of competition affecting industries. The five forces that shape the competitive environment amount to: the level of rivalry among competitors; the bargaining power of suppliers; the bargaining power of buyers; the threat of substitutes, and the threat of new entrants. Applying this framework to industry is aimed at strengthening competitive advantage. The analysis examines the intensity of competition and how concentrated the market is; how much power suppliers have in setting prices and controlling resources; the buying power of consumers and the level of differentiation in the industry; how easy or difficult it is for new companies to set up business in the industry; and how easy it is for consumers to switch vendors. Companies can use this analysis to find product-market positions and exercise bargaining power over suppliers and customers, and to exclude or block new entrants and rivals from its position (Küng, 2017). An often-raised criticism against this framework, however, is that it is largely tailored to highly stable markets and defined sectors, and consequently its appropriateness to the platform economy is reduced.

Structure-Conduct-Performance analyses of industry sectors are performed by breaking up the three elements and operationalising them. The structure of a market is defined by the number of buyers and sellers present and the amount of concentration among them; the degree of product differentiation and the presence of brand preferences in consumers; the existence of barriers to entry and whether these are controlled through cost structures or regulation; the extent of vertical integration in an industry, and the existence of or move towards conglomerates. Conduct can be assessed by looking at the behaviour of firms in the realm of pricing, products, advertising, and research and development. Performance assessments amount to questions of profitability, efficiency in production and resource allocation, employment and income distribution, and the diversity of content or products. The Structure-Conduct-Performance framework thus works to explain the relationship between various forms of market structure and firm behaviour (Van Kranenburg & Hogenbrink, 2006).

A competing theory of competitive advantage takes the firm as its starting point rather than the market structure. The Resource-Based View (RBV) (Barney, 1991) assumes that sustainable competitive advantage can be gained from resources that are unique – hereunder the core resources of the firm that are valuable, rare, non-substitutable, and difficult to imitate (Mauri & Michaels, 1998). This framework assumes that each firm is a collection of unique resources that enable them to conceive and implement strategies that lead to sustainable competitive advantage (Baumann, 2020; Chan-Olmsted, 2006; Mierzejewska, 2011). There are many ways to classify a firm's resources, but they largely fall into two categories as either property-based resources or knowledge-based resources, including a firm's physical resources, human resources, and organisational resources. Hereunder, valuable resources "only become *resources* when they exploit opportunities or neutralize threats in a firm's environment" (Barney, 1991, p. 106). Barney thus defines competitive advantage as "implementing a value creating strategy not simultaneously being implemented by any current or potential competitors" (ibid., p. 102); and sustained competitive advantage as when other firms are unable "to duplicate the benefits of this strategy" (ibid.).

Both the Resource-Based View of competitive advantage and the Structure-Conduct-Performance framework have been criticised in media research. The Structure-Conduct-Performance model has, in particular, been criticised for assuming linear causalities from structure to conduct to performance, when in fact these conditions are hardly stable in media markets (Flew, 2012; Van Kranenburg & Hogenbrink, 2006). Both frameworks have also been criticised for focusing too narrowly on the industry level, whereas competition in media markets often extends across industries (Dimmick, 2006; Picard & Lowe, 2016). Media management research has therefore largely shifted away from the Industrial Organisation perspective in recent years and towards more adaptive and interpretive approaches (Chan-Olmsted, 2006).

The field of media management studies is closely allied to media economics, but with a focus more attuned to external forces such as technology, regulation, and consumption over questions of firm performance (Küng, 2007). It emerged in the late 1990s and early 2000s as organisational culture came to be seen as a root cause for the media's failure to adapt to digitalisation (Mierzejewska & Hollifield, 2006). Classic management research is about improving the means of production and worker productivity, whereas "strategic management is concerned with developing the tools and techniques to analyse industries and competitors and developing strategies to gain competitive advantage" (Albarran, 2006, p. 10). Media management research is more case-study-oriented than strategic management, focused on mid-level management, business models, and organisational architecture (Picard & Lowe, 2016). Media management literature has been preoccupied with issues such as value generation, synergy, innovation, and disruption. Most of the early literature in this field was optimistic about the possibilities that management innovation could afford. Many scholars were keen to attain industry impact with their research, encouraging news managers to be entrepreneurial and flexible, to embrace new technology and market opportunities, and to focus on product development and innovation. And all this despite the fact that, as Küng (2007) notes, media management research has not seemed to matter unduly to the industry.

Media management research employs mainly three conceptual frameworks: rationalist approaches including the Industrial Organisation framework with the Structure-Conduct-Performance paradigm; adaptive approaches which view strategy as an ongoing process; and interpretive approaches where cognitive and unconscious aspects such as culture and bounded rationality are seen to matter (Küng, 2011). However, overviews of media management studies tend to be rather self-critical on behalf of the field, and often characterise scholarship here as under-theorised (Küng, 2016), unsystematic (Mierzejewska, 2011), and limited in methodology (Picard & Lowe, 2016). Küng (2016) has identified the challenge here as the application of theory from a wide set of disciplines to a diverse set of industries undergoing extreme change. Technologies have always been a management challenge, as their effects are non-linear and unpredictable (Küng, 2007), but the impact of the technology sector on media industries makes things more complicated, changing the competitive landscape. In addition, media industries are in the business of creating content, the demand for which is constantly shifting. The organisational pressures on media industries thus consist of adaptability and creativity, both needed to develop new business models. To that end, says Albarran (2006) "The evolving nature of the communications industries hinders the adoption of a universal theory of media management" (p. 11).

Scholars in this field thus apply a range of theoretical approaches to understand transformations in the news industries including frameworks that consider the organisational characteristics of journalistic institutions. This includes dynamic capabilities theory (e.g., Kosterich, 2020) to understand how news organisations and professions adapt to change; agency theory (e.g., Sjøvaag et al., 2021) to examine how news managers deal with mergers and acquisitions; niche theory (e.g., Pantic, 2021) to analyse how local newspapers stay competitive; innovation theory to investigate how journalism adapts to change (cf. Belair-Gagnon & Steinke, 2020); and the conditions needed for entrepreneurialism to be successful in the news industries (e.g., O'Brien & Wellbrock, 2021). Media management perspectives thus lend themselves rather well to examining stability and change in the news industries, not least because management research includes organisational and thus institutional perspectives that allow for a more holistic approach to journalism within the framework of news as a business. To that end, media management research is decidedly more concerned about what works in the context of industry survival than the critical political economy tradition (cf. Rohn & Evens, 2020), which is less concerned with solutions than it is with problem definitions.

Sociology versus economics

The two broad directions understand the business of journalism differently. That is, they have opposite views of the function that economic structures and arrangements bear on the news industries. On the question of money, management research considers it an attainable resource – you just have to find the best strategy to get it (or keep it but definitely not lose it), and to align your resource utilisation to sustain it. For critical political economy, money is the profit motive that leads to inequality, exploitation, and the unfair distribution of welfare. Likewise, ownership is a resource in management terms, while owners are profit driven exploiters of labour in critical political economy. In media management, control is important to manage costs and resources, while in critical research, control is subversive on expression, freedom, and diversity. Power is something you need in a market to sustain your competitive advantage, while power in critical scholarship is what counteracts democracy. Convergence, innovation, and disruption are more likely to be seen as economic processes in critical political economy (cf. Murdock & Golding, 2002), while they tend to be viewed as technological processes from a media economics and management viewpoint.

These stark differences stem from the intellectual histories of the two fields. Whereas Marx viewed capitalism as the system that takes power away from the workers, benefitting the owners of the means of production, Adam Smith believed enlightened self-interest would ensure the fair distribution of welfare. Both directions, however, reject this idea that markets can be free and self-regulated, largely because of the public good characteristics of media products. Both also dismiss Smith's benevolent belief that consumers' self-interest necessarily includes consideration for the needs of others – this also rooted in the merit good characteristics of cultural products. This is perhaps where media and journalism research can be 'pure' political economy – in the examination of media industries as sites and institutions for the production of goods that society needs. There are also emerging topics of interest that mobilise political economic frameworks with a less critical flair, such as infrastructure studies and studies of the information society, but that still temper what Winseck (2017) has called the techno-utopian views of the internet as advanced by scholars like Yochai Benkler (2002) and Lawrence Lessig (2002) in the early days of the internet. In fact, critical political economy perspectives have over the past few years moved outside the Western sphere of research, more commonly found in research on post-Soviet Europe, Africa, and Asian media systems (e.g., Ambelu et al., 2021; Kim, 2018). Critical perspectives are also more readily available in cultural industries and in critical media industries studies (e.g., Havens et al., 2012), as well as in research on creative labour and media work (Holt & Perren, 2019).

As for the issue of disruption, both research traditions are worried about the sustainability of journalism and its democratic functions. For instance, Iris Chyi (2013) has criticised the news industries in the U.S. for buying into tech-optimistic Silicon Valley jargon and for neglecting their most valued product, the printed newspaper (see also Bell et al., 2017). Industry trends and terms have thus tended to move into the research field rather than the other way around. Media industries, business and management perspectives have, nevertheless, become more central in media research due to the fact that digitalisation and the move to AI disrupt exactly this part of the journalistic institution – its management and organisation, business models, and strategies. Media management, journalism, and organisational research are here less concerned with the enduring forms of journalistic production than they are about new ways of doing things – lean thinking, entrepreneurialism, innovation, dynamic capabilities – while they often find newsrooms to be rather resistant to change. There might indeed be better and smarter ways to organise and manage news production, yet the newsroom as organisational form endures.

As for critical political economy, the monopoly capitalism perspective that considers the impact of concentration in the communications industries on democracy and culture has carried through to platform, internet, and data studies. Scholars have begun to interrogate the impact of infrastructure on the news industries (Braun & Eklund, 2019; Winseck, 2017), the role of platforms in the media ecology (Bode & Vraga, 2018; Ruotsalainen & Heinonen, 2015), and consider news media as multi-sided markets rather than two-sided markets (Gabszewicz et al., 2015). This is not least due to the impact of AI in the communications sector, and the power this yields to the platform players. Concentration and monopolisation thus remain an enduring and even increasing characteristic of the media and communications industries (Winseck, 2019). For news organisations in particular, chain formation seems to be a response to concentration in the tech industries. While niche strategies might be necessary to compete in the digital disruption, economies of scale still protect organisations from the most volatile changes in the communications sector.

The merits of political economy and media management in assessing the economic dimensions of journalism are clearly present. However, these perspectives also leave a few things to be desired. Dimensions of power are of course important to understand the role of media and the many actors who perform functions in media industries. The distribution of communicative power in society is itself largely determined by the political and economic structure of society, including class relations and reception habits in audiences, the culture of ownership, and the level of professionalism in journalism. As I have argued elsewhere, however (Sjøvaag, 2019), in order to fully understand how news as product-markets shape the journalistic institution, money – as something that serves as a resource when you have it – and the mechanisms by which that resource is attained – the market economy in which news is traded – needs to be included in the institutional perspective on journalism. In doing the research required for this chapter, particularly in reading through research reviews and blindspot debates, there is something exhausting about these exercises. While they may be intent on creating impact, identity, and community, they are also inherently excluding, particularly to scholars who did not know, frankly, that sides existed or that there is indeed a need to take sides. There is an empirical reality, and the appropriate way to study it depends on the research question, not a pre-existing answer, whether it be that capitalism is to blame or that innovation is the way to succeed. So, let's try a more analytical approach to the question of news markets and the place of economics in journalism, by applying the theoretical perspective of new economic sociology – one that acknowledges that the economy in fact is "very important" (Swedberg et al., 1987, p. 170) in society, and thus that economic action is embedded in social reality.

A third option: sociological and institutional economics

Rational choice theories have not been extensively applied in journalism studies. A few offshoots from rational choice perspectives are, however, particularly relevant, specifically in terms of how institutions are discussed and in how agency is perceived. For instance, Hallin and Mancini (2004) have based their media systems typology on the concept of path dependency derived from Douglas North (1990). North's book on *Institutions, Institutional Change and Economic Performance*, presents a key framework for institutional theory. His sports metaphor, for instance, has often been mobilised to explain the difference between organisations and institutions – the field and its rules being the institution and the teams the organisations who try to win by following the rules. Path dependency, to North, explains how incremental changes in technology, once embarked upon, can lead one technology to succeed even if a competing technology is more efficient. Path dependency therefore links decision-making through time. North (1990) says that "Once a development path is set on a particular course, the network externalities, the learning process of organizations, and the historically derived subjective modelling of the issues reinforce the course" (p. 99). Path dependency also explains how institutions adapt to external changes *at the margins*, and how implemented changes tend to build on already existing institutional arrangements. Institutions are resistant to change, but when they do change, they protect their core, while the changes that are made are implemented based on already established routines and rules.

As journalism faces disruption, then, both in technology and competition, the steps taken to ensure survival, or competitive advantage, are harder to implement at the core – in its ownership form, newsroom organisation or journalistic professionalism – than at the fringes of the news operation. Moreover, the decisions made along the way create a basis for the next decision. The business model innovations that newspapers have engaged with have been geared towards additional revenue streams rather than a complete revamp of its two-sided economic model. In addition, path dependency explains why news organisations, once they have embarked on partnerships with platform intermediaries, find them difficult to withdraw from.

New institutionalist theories like North's (1990) path dependency proceed from the assumption that humans are neither completely rational nor completely irrational. Instead, agents operate under a bounded rationality where decision-making is constrained by various factors and conditions that limit the information available to them (Kahneman, 2011; Thomas, 2016). The concept of bounded rationality has been used to explain how journalism meets uncertainty (Lowrey & Gade, 2011), how journalists face innovation processes (Slot, 2021), and how CEOs manage risk (Sjøvaag et al., 2021). Particularly in a rapidly changing economic and technological landscape, decision-making in the news industries is constrained not only by limited information about the future; decisions are also bound by the goals and rules of the institution itself. Hence, when managers and CEOs are forced to set strategies and priorities within a limited information space, they look both to their core values and resources, and to the actions and strategies of their competitors. Expanding the holdings of the company through chain formation not only increases the data available to managers on which to take decisions in such turbulent circumstances, it also mitigates risk when experiments can be made at the margins, lowering the impact of failures on the core operation.

To that end, industry reaction to technological, economic, and political change occurs within what March & Olsen (1983) have termed a logic of appropriateness. The logic of appropriateness explains how the institutional environment shapes the agency of actors. This concept has been used to understand the implications of data journalism (Jamil, 2021), constructions of journalistic knowledge (Olsen, 2018), and decision-making within news organisations (Jääsaari & Olson, 2010). According to the logic of appropriateness, action is determined by the situation at hand, the social system in which it occurs, and is influenced by socialisation processes that shape agents' behaviours (March & Olsen, 1983). This logic stands in contrast to a logic of consequence, where choices and actions are based on expected outcomes. A logic of appropriateness assumes that decisions are more based on following rules and fulfilling identities (Olsson, 2009). The economic actions of news organisations thus happen within a space of appropriateness determined by the culture of the organisation, the ownership form and thus the types of control that owners can assert, the relationship of the news organisation to the state, and the professional norms and normative expectations of journalism that agents operate under.

As Granovetter (1985) explains, economic action is embedded in social relations. These relations constitute structures or networks that generate trust, or conversely, that can generate malfeasance. Markets should therefore also be understood as organisational contexts where cultural frames contribute to shape the social relations between actors (Fligstein, 2001). Organisations are also embedded in markets as socially constructed arenas that shape how information is transmitted, how operational standards are defined, and how trust is generated (Fligstein & Calder, 2015). As these relationships constitute networks, the rules set by the leading industry players contribute to shape the rules governing the entire industry (ibid.). The concept of embeddedness thus contributes to explaining the problems facing the news industries as social media platforms move in to assume the key positions in the information economy on which journalism relies.

The next chapter examines this problem in detail, analysing the effects of the properties of platforms on the journalism industries.

5 Platform power

Two things in particular challenge journalism's two-sided business model as a framework for understanding how news makes money: platforms and networks. These features make media markets multi-sided markets where network effects enable scale, lock-in, and monopoly positions. They also upset the established value chain of production. In a traditional value chain, value accumulates up the chain, from material resources through production and assembly to distribution. While the Resource-Based View (Barney, 1991) says that competitive advantage comes from controlling scarce and inimitable assets, a platform's resource lie with the network of producers and consumers that constitutes its community. The chief assets of platforms are thus information and interactions. As Van Alstyne and colleagues (2016) describe it, industrial economics is driven by supply-side economies of scale. This means high fixed costs and low marginal costs. Higher volume means lower average cost, which allows for reducing prices, increasing volume further, which permits price cuts, producing monopolies. Market power in the industrial economy is thus achieved by controlling resources, increasing efficiency, and fending off challengers. The main strategy here is to defend the business from competition. The driving force of the internet economy, on the other hand, is demand-side economies of scale, or network effects. Technologies create efficiencies to expand networks. Higher volume in the form of more participants offers higher value per transaction. Hence, the larger the network the better the matches between supply and demand and the richer the data to find matches. Greater scale generates more value, creating monopolies (ibid.). To that end, platforms economics constitute an entirely different set of principles that challenge the business model for news.

Platforms replace two-sided market structures with multi-sided configurations (Nieborg & Poell, 2018). A platform is software or hardware infrastructure where users, companies, and governments build applications, services, and communities (Casilli & Posada, 2019). These are

DOI: 10.4324/9781003081791-5

complementary technologies that mediate the production, search, and delivery of digital content among users. They host, organise, and circulate content and social interactions without having produced most of that content (Gillespie, 2018). Because users transact with each other at the same time as they transact with the platform, the value shifts from the chain to the network (Karimi & Walter, 2015).

Platforms are programmable, modular, and rule-based architectures (Gawer, 2014; Helmond, 2015; Van Alstyne et al., 2016; Van Dijck et al., 2018) that are open to regulated participation (Parker et al., 2016). They provide the technical standards, connectivity, IT capabilities, and rules and social norms that enable multiple firms to develop complementary products, technologies, and services (Coyle, 2018). Hence, they often have privileged positions in their industries, as other participants rely on them in important ways (Hagiu, 2014). As they are open-ended, they support further development and benefit from increased interaction and data. A platform's value creation thus consists of encoding (producing user traces such as likes, browsing, ranking, friending), aggregation (creating aggregates of traced actions) and computation (using algorithms to find patterns) (Beaulieu & Leonelli, 2022). As most platforms rely on advertising, this drives much of their design and policy decision-making. To better target this advertising, says Gillespie (2018) "platforms are oriented toward data collection and retention, toward eliciting more data, and more kinds of data, from its users; and toward finding new ways to draw users to the platform, and to follow users off platform wherever they may go" (p. 19). Hence, platforms have two important functions: datafication and programmability. They serve as sites for data generation and combination, and they support the development of applications and organise user participation.

Platforms provide data access through Application Programming Interfaces (APIs) and Software Development Kits (SDKs) that enable data to move between different software. Essentially, APIs allow applications to communicate. These tools provide a stable environment that allows for consistency and replicability of coding (McIntyre & Srinivasan, 2017). A platform's infrastructure thus lowers the cost of innovation because there is no need to build a new system every time (Plantin et al., 2018). APIs can also be seen, then, as regulatory instruments that govern the relations between platforms and third parties. They are essentially the business model of the social web. As Helmond (2015) explains, APIs enable third parties to add value to the platform by building services on top of it through data exchange and modularisation of content and features. APIs allow for a dual logic in this regard – expansion onto the rest of the web and making external websites and apps platform ready. Nieborg and Poell (2018) argue that this entails a "process of infrastructural alignment" (p. 4288), as websites need to configure their data to fit the design and agenda of the platform. Platforms are thus geared for lock-in (Plantin et al., 2018), whereby companies, websites, and complementors become dependent on the platform to reach users, and where finding alternatives entails high switching costs.

Platforms enable strong network effects. A fundamental premise of platform-mediated networks is that users place higher value on networks with large numbers of users. Network effects can be direct or indirect. Direct network effects occur when the benefit of user participation depends on the number of users they can interact with (McIntyre & Srinivasan, 2017). Indirect network effects occur when the value of one side increases with the number of participants on the other (Hagiu, 2014). The different sides of the network thus enjoy mutual benefits from the size and characteristics of the other side. The presence of strong indirect network effects means that users joining or leaving the platform indirectly affects the perceived value of the platform on the other side. Platforms thus face a *chicken and egg-problem*: no side will join without the other (Evans, 2003; Hagiu, 2015; Rieder & Sire, 2014).

To get people on board, platforms tend to strongly subsidise one group. One side of the market typically covers the cost of the more price-sensitive side (Coyle, 2018). This is a common feature in multi-sided markets – that most of the revenue comes from one side. Typical examples here include American Express, which earns most of its revenue from merchants, and Microsoft, which gets the bulk of its income from license buyers (Evans, 2003). Multi-homing is therefore common in platform markets, whereby both consumers and suppliers will use multiple platforms. Operating systems prevent multi-homing, as users only use one operating system, while developers tend to multi-home, often delivering solutions to multiple systems. Platforms that have single-homing on one side and multi-homing on the other often create competitive bottlenecks (Coyle, 2018), and tend towards monopoly (Beaulieu & Leonelli, 2022). In the news industries, newspapers normally have multi-homing on both sides of the market. Most readers use more than one source for news, and most advertisers use multiple channels for exposure. This puts newspapers in a weak position as platform competitors sweep in to assume the platform function linking audiences and advertisers that newspapers used to have in the past.

Platforms are therefore not like traditional firms. They act more like meta-organisations or marketplaces that transcend the original boundaries of the firm. For one thing, platforms use algorithms to coordinate their components rather than pricing. Supply and demand are matched algorithmically, the peer mechanisms for which serve to lower information asymmetry (Coyle, 2018). Labour on a platform is often taskified and outsourced (Casilli & Posada, 2019). Their human resources tend to reside in external communities rather than internal employees (Parker et al., 2016). As such, they do not act as employers *per se* (Beaulieu & Leonelli, 2022). Platforms also tend not to produce the products and services they provide. Value creation has therefore moved beyond the direct control of the company. Even marketing can be outsourced to users. Hence, platforms shed the variable costs of production (Van Alstyne et al., 2016). Their core business is to provide information about customers to vendors and information about vendors to customers. This is a business model based on the extraction, analysis, and monetising of personal data (Hintz et al., 2018). Platforms are thus not about controlling resources or increasing customer value but about orchestrating resources, facilitating external interactions, and maximising ecosystem value. Hence, the main product of platforms is the community.

In a sense, platforms here display the audience commodity in its purest form. For traditional media, as Smythe (1977) argued, the audience served media's function in four ways: in creating consumerism, in confirming the ideology of monopoly capitalism, in producing a supportive public opinion, and in gaining economic importance through profitability. The same can be said for the platform ecosystem. Platforms perform these functions through the user commodity. They create consumerism as algorithms are geared towards matching supply and demand and by linking content with users based on community ratings. They confirm the ideology of monopoly capitalism as scale facilitates network quality, creating monopolistic network effects and lock-in. They produce a supportive public opinion through algorithmically curated content environments based on popularity and virality. Their centrality as marketplaces connecting users and markets makes them important in the digital economy. In fact, their technical features and practices create market control (Jordan, 2020). To that end, audience and advertising revenue are not separable in the platform economy, as Murdock (1978) argued for the media industries. Users are still the commodity that advertisers seek, but users also provide the content alongside which advertising is placed. Network effects ensure that the value of the platform increases with the number of possible matches that can be made on the platform. This network effect used to belong to the media – providing eyeballs for advertisers. Now, journalism is just one form of content alongside all other content, substitutable as well as dispensable to the goal of user retention.

Journalism's response to the platform economy

Convergence theory once predicted that the media would merge with other sectors into one big sector. Instead, Küng (2017) notes, it seems more like the media is being swallowed by the tech sector. Bell (2016) even says of social media that it "hasn't just swallowed journalism, it has swallowed everything". This power shift has been noted by many scholars (e.g., Ekström & Westlund, 2019), whether it refers to the role of platforms as gatekeepers (Russell, 2019), the role of algorithms in shaping editorial decisions (Peterson-Salahuddin & Diakopoulos, 2020), or journalism's dependence on platforms to reach audiences (Kleis Nielsen & Ganter, 2018). Particularly the social media logic (Klinger & Svensson, 2015) and its elements of programmability, popularity, connectivity, and datafication (Van Dijck & Poell, 2013), are seen to impact editorial priorities (Nieborg & Poell, 2018) and journalistic style (Haim et al., 2021; Welbers & Opgenhaffen, 2019). The logics and affordances of platform distribution thus contribute to shape the economic model of news (Foster, 2012) as well as the quality of journalism. Because Google and Facebook provide the majority of audiences for news (Nechushtai, 2018), these platforms also constitute sources of growth, affecting news strategies and priorities. What they offer is reach, especially to younger audiences (Kleis Nielsen & Ganter, 2018). Power has therefore shifted from production to distribution (Siapera, 2013), with little leverage left for content providers. Moreover, as Bell and colleagues (2017) note, on platforms there is no premium for quality information, only scale. This puts platform economics fundamentally at odds with the public and merit good quality of news.

As Kleis Nielsen and Ganter (2018) observe, news media have engaged with digital intermediaries at every opportunity. Because platforms mediate most of the audience–journalism relationship, the news industries need to adjust by making their content platform ready (Russell, 2019). Nieborg and Poell (2018) see this as a move towards complementarity – ensuring content is modular, alterable, and optimised for platform monetisation. This entails a move from a linear production to an iterative, data-driven process where content is constantly altered to optimise for platform distribution. Scholars have characterised this development as platform dependence (ibid.) or infrastructure capture (Nechushtai, 2018) – a situation in which it becomes impossible to operate without the services of the platforms. In this context, Chan-Olmsted (2019) has noted that the real potential of AI for the news industries lies in developing competencies, not just acquiring new technologies. In the U.S. context, AI has been used mostly to improve content recommendations, automate workflows, help reporters find stories through intelligent agents, and allow for commercial optimisation through ad targeting and dynamic pricing. News media also use content management to improve metadata to facilitate faster content search and securing content quality (e.g., by searching for errors). They also use automated writing technologies to generate stories from data. To Chan-Olmsted (ibid.), the value of AI to news media thus lies more with functional and operational improvements than total replacement, not least because journalism is still a human exercise. Adapting news organisations' infrastructures to the needs of AI is, however, demanding for most smaller media.

Scholarship has approached journalism's platform dependency from multiple angles. While materiality perspectives such as Actor-Network theory have been applied mainly to newsroom studies of technological application and innovation in journalistic processes (cf. Anderson & De Maeyer, 2015; Boczkowski, 2009; Domingo, 2015; Moran & Usher, 2021; Neff, 2015), socio-technical theory has also been mobilised to understand how journalism meets the platform ecology and its technological features (Dörr, 2018). These perspectives focus on the interplay between humans and technology. Media industries studies have also employed material theories on issues such as circulation, practice, and labour (e.g., Postigo, 2016; Siles & Boczkowski, 2012). More recently, media industries scholars have begun to engage with distribution issues (Herbert et al., 2019; Donders, 2019) to understand the role of platforms and algorithms in media dissemination and use. Researchers have also moved towards infrastructure studies (Flensburg & Lai, 2020; Winseck, 2017) to expand the ecology in which media systems can be understood. Research is thus moving towards more diverse perspectives to comprehend how the social, political, and economic aspects of technology systems impact on the media industries. Importantly, scholars are beginning to acknowledge the limitation of mono-disciplinary approaches to these topics.

There is, however, a notable return to critical perspectives. Whereas critical political economy scholars from the mass media era saw the economy as operating on two levels – the capitalist as well as the cultural level – this perspective is increasingly applied to technology, whereby datafication, algorithmisation, and programmability are recognised as political, and thus ideological, processes (Casilli & Posada, 2019; Gillespie, 2010). Many have revisited Marx in the context of creative labour and media work in the digital economy (Holt & Perren, 2019), often considering digital labour to be both precarious and exploitative in nature (Nieborg & Poell, 2018). The critical political economy perspective has also been applied to the impact of corporate ownership on the platform sector, particularly as it refers to the accumulative tendency of capital and its effect on the distribution of power (ibid.). Platforms are seen to commodify information, increasing the importance of surveillance practices and centralised control over information, leading to what Andrejevic (2007) has termed "digital enclosure". Mobilising critical political economic theory to understand this shift in power has shed important light on the impact of platform technologies and ontologies on the media ecology at large. Moreover, this perspective has been useful in understanding how the strategies and aims of platforms impact on 'complementary' industries. Media industries research has been rather responsive to this shift, examining what this new competitive landscape and its resources mean for the news industry (cf. McDonald, 2022).

A weakness in the critical political economy framework, Nieborg & Poell (2018) note, is that critical approaches tend to overlook the role of infrastructures, the multi-sidedness of markets and their network effects, as well as the governance systems that rule them. There is thus a limit to how useful the critical political economy focus on cultural practices, consumption, and symbolic form is for understanding how technology shifts power within the economic ecosystem of digital media. A more non-critical application of political economic theory, particularly its focus on the distribution of resources and economic and political power structures in society, has been fruitfully applied to digital infrastructures and how they impact media access and use. As Flensburg and Lai (2020) explain, political economy is useful for identifying key actors in this system, and how they control the development, organisation, and distribution of resources in the context of existing power structures. Political economy as the study of relations between markets and states, wealth distribution, and governance systems thus contains the type of perspectives that can account for the impact of market principles and realities and how they shape behaviour within the system.

To properly identify and study the resources within the platform economy, however, I would argue that a media economics perspective is also useful, as it allows for identifying values and assets within the system. When combined with economic sociology, these resources can be conceptualised as value streams within networks governed by a certain logic. Including economic sociology can thus help to offset some of the limitations of economic theory, particularly the economic framework's presupposition of stability. Economic theory also tends to overlook the impact of platform design and usually limits competition analysis to specific platforms rather than looking broadly at platform ecosystems (Gawer, 2014). Studying platform effects on the media ecosystem is made difficult because of these limitations. Access to data is cumbersome, particularly as it pertains to systems design and competition, not least because much of this data is proprietary.

Overall, analyses of the platform ecosystem in which the news media operate are made difficult by the multi-sidedness of markets, the abundance of content, the multiplicity of use situations, and the shift in value creation that platforms and networks afford. Defining the competitive space also becomes complicated as markets expand globally. Applying established competition policy to platform markets is, moreover, problematic because markets are less separate than they used to be, for instance in the case of search and advertising (Coyle, 2018), or diversity (Sjøvaag, 2014b). With new entrants emerging rapidly and incumbents moving fast into new markets with little warning (Van Alstyne et al., 2016), the competitive landscape tends to shift rapidly, making it hard to establish a firm grip on competitors, strategies, and their resources. The political economy of communication has had a tendency to examine media markets separately, to focus only on national media, and to look to the state to solve the problem of media's economic sustainability. While dynamics of power still play out within these dimensions, the dominance of platforms and their logics supersede the agency that national regulations have in controlling the information space in which citizens operate. From whatever angle we approach this issue, a more expansive theoretical framework is needed.

The explanatory power of theory

If political economy is about applying the logics of economics to political phenomena (Swedberg, 2006), then understanding the networked platform ecology and its governance should involve questions of resource distribution, value creation and labour organisation. As we have seen, however, platform economics is not like industrial economics. Labour is not organised, resources constitute connections rather than products, and value is produced by data rather than prices. As for the relationship between the state and the market and how the two forces influence individuals, groups, and society at large, states have demonstrated little power in controlling these markets or even the principles by which trade occurs within these networks. The markets created by the platforms are instead seen to shape the laws and norms that govern interaction within the digital economy. Seen in this light, structural inequalities are directly generated by the technological infrastructure of platforms themselves. In the view of critical political economy, then, platform economics affects political and social power to the extent that it constitutes a problem for society. Not only are the platforms both dominant and commercial, their networked and multi-sided infrastructures create monopoly positions that should indeed raise concerns regarding their effects on cultural production and the circulation of meaning.

The 'critical' perspective in political economy was largely developed for and applied to dominant, commercial media and their power in shaping culture and society. This perspective was developed when media were rich and the wealth of these dominant commercial players predominantly came from another commercial activity, namely advertising. Money was something entirely different to the media industries within the industrial economy than it is within the platform economy. From holding dominant, non-substitutable platform positions within a two-sided market, media within the platform economy is merely one of many substitutable content providers in a multi-sided marketplace. The critical perspective that saw media power as a potential risk to democracy is of course still relevant in contexts where media companies are primarily commercially or politically motivated. However, there is a larger perspective at work here where platform economics offers an opportunity for critical scholarship to extend the political economy of communications to the platform level, applying the critical framework to examine how the platforms themselves influence existing class and social relations.

In this context, media, and in particular journalistic and editorial media, have a subservient role, in which case they should perhaps be championed and supported as conduits of democratic oversight and participation, rather than seen with suspicion as protectors of the ideological status quo. Moving the suspicion with which critical political economic scholarship views capitalist power to the platform level may not necessarily detract from the potentially negative effects of big media on the circulation of meaning. However, it should also be clear that as the power to control public communication shifts to the platform level, the sites of struggles over issues like social justice, resistance, and emancipation no longer reside within the media ecology alone. The media system includes infrastructural players whose logics and economics change the rules of the game. As the economic logics of the platform ecology follows the algorithmic logic, the alignment of cultural production to logics and affordances beyond industrial economics should be acknowledged. Media does not have the power it once had. Critical political economic theory should adjust to this reality.

Media economics of course faces the same types of issues as the political economy of communication. If media economics is the study of how the media uses scarce resources to produce content and bring it to market, then this market space no longer contains clear separations between markets and industries, blurred in large part by algorithmic processing. Existing theories that explain competitive advantage within this realm are faced with new questions concerning how resources are defined within the platform ecology, and how they can be controlled. The inclusion of management theory into the study of media industries thus shifts the focus away from external factors and questions of how to leverage or mitigate outside factors onto how to manage resources internally and how to adapt to rapidly changing environments. There is a limit, however, to how flexible an industry can be when most strategies are focused on adaptation to attain the "infrastructure alignment" (Nieborg & Poell, 2018) that platforms require. The principles of creativity and creative labour that support the production of cultural products also face new challenges. The ontologies of networks that match producers with consumers are not only governed by a logic of popularity; they also entail an economy in which audiences become producers of content. It is difficult to see exactly how media industries are supposed to innovate their way out of the "capture" (Nechushtai, 2018) that platforms represent to their business model. To what extent the news industries can use AI technologies to develop their organisational capabilities in this new economy also remains to be seen. So far, it seems AI adaptation is largely reactive according to the alignment thesis rather than entrepreneurial to the point where news organisations can get ahead of the platforms in securing audience attention.

The two frameworks of critical political economy and media management have opposing views on the function that economic structures and arrangements have on news industries. If management is about finding the best strategy to align resource utilisation to sustain income, it is not surprising that researchers find AI application for platform alignment to be the dominant strategy. This is a technical process that changes journalistic production and dissemination logics in a way that challenges the editorial and curatorial philosophies of the media industries. Two competing logics of appropriateness are therefore present in news organisations which find themselves operating within the platform ecology. One is the journalistic and editorial logic of appropriateness that rests on professional ethics and social contract norms where the news should ideally assist citizens in monitoring the powers in society. The other is the algorithmic logic of scalability and programmability that subscribes to the logic of popularity. While the managerial logic in journalism must adhere to the logic of professionalism within the field, the institutional logic of commercial media also includes an economic logic where survival is imperative to fulfil journalism's purpose. Media management perspectives are thus more sensitive to the issue of industry survival – issues that shape companies' strategies – than the critical political economy of communication. The issue here is to what extent agents' bounded rationality within the media industries is shaped by the logics of the platforms, and how this affects journalism as product and profession.

The institutional perspectives that apply sociological theory to economic phenomena thus offer a pathway to understanding the dilemmas facing news managers in the move towards the platform economy. While scholars have observed that news managers seem to have engaged with the platforms at every opportunity, in the spirit of "let's try it and see" (Kleis Nielsen & Ganter, 2018), decision-making within the news industries is also highly constrained by uncertainty. News managers have limited information about the future, limited information about the platforms, limited feedback from the data they are able to garner from the application of AI in news production, and limited information about the potential success of costly innovation processes. In fact, most news managers' information is limited to what they can observe in their competitors in the news industries. At the same time, managers operate under a bounded rationality where decision-making must align with the core values of the institution. Those core values are not only editorial – they are also economic. Media are also businesses, and economic considerations are part of the institutional thinking that supports journalism as an enterprise. This does not mean that journalism first and foremost has an economic logic of appropriateness. Rather, the economic and material conditions of journalism are influenced by social processes (Fligstein, 2015). That is, the economics of journalism must be seen in its social context.

As Swedberg (2006) asserts, economic action is social action. It is first and foremost interest that drives economic action, while social relations give them direction. Swedberg thus conceptualises institutions as "dominant models for how interests can be realized" (2006, p. 12). Institutions form the rationality context in which actors pursue interests. In other words, in order to realise interest, agents need to orient their behaviour to the relevant institution. Society thus consists of ongoing activities that form institutions in action. These actions in turn form the power of institutions. Hence, there is a limit to what kind of economic action is acceptable with the journalistic institution. Making money with journalistic content is acceptable, but there is also contestation surrounding certain forms of revenue generation in journalism, such as native advertising. Opening up editorial spaces, not least journalistic forms and genres, to commercial messages disguised as journalism has been met with criticism from both inside and outside journalism. The interest that drives this action is motivated by the pursuit of profit to sustain the core editorial product. Likewise, the alignment of news outlets to programmatic advertising through the generation of audience data and algorithmic curation, is motivated by economic incentives to adjust to the needs of the advertising sector to generate income. This is less fraught with tension, as this economic action is more in line with the logic of appropriateness concerning the separation of news and commerce in the traditional newspaper format.

The issue of infrastructure alignment, on the other hand – making content complementary and platform ready to enable data utilisation to suit the economic interests of social media platforms – is another issue altogether. These processes are to a lesser extent under the control of editors, journalists, and news managers than economically motivated actions towards the advertising industry – a sector with which journalism has a longstanding, established, and thus more institutional relationship. As journalism becomes more dependent on the procedural logics of AI technologies, this presents a growing contradiction with the editorial logics that drives the essential interest of the institution (cf. Gillespie, 2014). Here, the logics of platform economics represents an interest struggle – one that remains largely out of reach of the institutional interests of journalism. Journalism does not operate so much in a social context in this case, but in a technological context, representing material conditions influenced by the economic interests of the platform ecology where what counts as acceptable economic behaviour remains at odds with the premises of the economic foundations of the media industries.

Journalism thus remains in a transitional phase. The disruption continues. As Newman and colleagues at the Reuters Institute for the Study of Journalism have demonstrated through their annual Digital News Reports dating back to 2012, the news industries are mainly reactive to these ongoing processes. However, to understand the altered landscape in which journalism manoeuvres, it is imperative that we understand the economic principles at play, and how they affect an industry's strategy and management. As this chapter has hopefully demonstrated, platform economics is different from industrial economics. This shift constitutes in large part the struggles that journalism experiences in its business model foundation. However, for all the adaptation and alignment that goes on in the news industries, journalism still subscribes to an institutional logic. This logic too, is at odds with the logics of platforms. These two disruptions are thus intertwined. If interest drives economic action, the question is what kind of social relation gives this interest direction. As the network of relations expands, interest alignment also changes.

6 Conclusions

Journalism is about the production of news, and news is a commodity sold in a marketplace. However, news is not like other products, and news markets are not like other markets. News is a creative product with public good qualities and positive externalities. It has value beyond its unit cost and direct utility. News has societal value. If there is no money to be made from producing news in the commercial sector, there will likely be less of it, and it will likely be of poorer quality. The absence of news will impact negatively on society and its citizens. If we are to have news, a profitable news industry is imperative. The state cannot, essentially, subsidise all the journalists whose jobs require them to oversee power. Journalism needs independence from the state to legitimately monitor state power. As making news costs money, revenue has to be sought in the market, where market rules apply.

There are two markets for news – one market where news is sold to audiences and one market where the audiences for news are sold to advertisers. Journalism is the platform connecting the two markets. In both cases, news used to be a non-substitutable product. Social media and online search have introduced a third market, the networked platform market, where news is but one of many products on offer, substitutable both to the platforms and their advertisers. This platform market has been identified as the main growth potential for news (Küng, 2017). Hence, the market where news is but one commodity in competition with other types of content has shifted the competitive advantage of journalism to the point where adaptability to complement the economics of platforms is key. Crucially, in this new market, someone else is also making money off news – the platforms. This amounts to free-riding, whereby the platforms are able to capitalise on the investments made in the news industries to attract users to their networks.

When public goods face too much free-riding, it can lead to market failure. Market failure is a problem because it means that private interest pursuits have disrupted the fair distribution of resources that society needs.

DOI: 10.4324/9781003081791-6

Typically in these instances, the state intervenes to either regulate markets or subsidise merit goods. As it stands, this option is difficult for many states in the case of market failure for news. Not only is there a limit to how much journalism states can reasonably subsidise; there is also a jurisdictional limit to their ability to regulate the platform markets. While news media are certainly lobbying governments for increased protection and support from this market disruption, they are also making adjustments to reduce costs. There is, however, a limited number of options available for news organisations to save money. News production is a costly business. When profits are down, costs must follow. A typical way to offset costs is to spread it on more units. The way to attain this effect is scale.

The subtitle of this book argues that journalism has certain enduring features that prevail in the context of digital disruptions. Journalism has undergone continuous transformations towards the digital since the introduction of the internet. After nearly 30 years, much of what makes journalism "journalism" remains the same. News is still produced in newsrooms according to ethical norms and professional standards. Methods pretty much remain the same, with interviews, fact checking and documentation at the core of professional practice. Amateurs and citizens remain at the fringes of news production, and online commentary is largely monitored and curated. Newspapers still try to get readers to subscribe to ensure steady, predictable income, and they still try to attract advertising. As the need for technology increases, news organisations merge towards larger entities to engender scale to empower the data analytics needed to participate in the market for programmatic advertising. Hence, a two-sided market thinking remains in effect, established organisational solutions to attain scale prevail, and owners still, largely, expect a profit in return for their investment. While journalism is certainly undergoing continuous changes, organisational arrangements remain more or less constant. Many of these arrangements are economic in nature.

As we saw in the previous chapter, the economic principles on which news markets have rested are facing serious challenges in the move towards the platform economy. Platform economies are not like industrial economies. The value chain no longer accumulates value up the chain, instead value is created by linking users in the network. The users constitute the primary value, not the content. When newspapers put their news online in the first phase of digitalisation, it was a matter of moving content to another technology. As journalism adapts to social media, it is a process of adjusting content to a new set of affordances; owned and determined by a third party. The uneasiness with which news media relate to the platform players has begun to display signs of withdrawal from certain digital markets and environments, some news outlets dissolving or scaling back partnerships with social media players, and others seeking revenue from sources outside the platform sphere, such as trusts, foundations, and donations, as well as digital, direct audience revenue. There is a return to core values in the industry, including refocusing on trust, partnership, community, and membership in their relationship with audiences.

The economic thinking of the news industries thus displays strong path dependencies. News media are still thinking about how to generate revenue from audiences, and how to make those audiences valuable to advertisers. The high-risk environment in which journalism operates, and the limited information that news managers have about the future, only increases this path dependence further. However, continuous change also contributes to shape the belief system within the institutional space. Here, the dominant beliefs are often defined by the actors who are in a position to set the rules and norms that determine economic performance, revising the perception of reality of other players in the field (North, 1990). When researchers talk about the power of platforms in shaping culture (e.g., Gillespie, 2014), these institutional mechanisms are at play. New actors move in, take over, and alter norm alignment as a result. Moreover, once news media venture onto the path of AI analytics and optimisation, past investments tend to shape future strategies. Straying from the path that costly AI investments have enabled is thus less optimal than continuing to make further adjustments towards the platforms. The contradiction between the two economic realities that journalism operates within under the digital economy places the institution in a precarious position, where neither economy seems to provide the necessary income to sustain the industry.

This path dependency is of course also tied to the media system properties in which news media operate. The economic situation for journalism is not as dire in the Scandinavian region as it is in other media systems such as the U.S. or the U.K. Scandinavian news media enjoy higher levels of trust from its users, public service broadcasting remains strong, local news structures have so far endured, and news outlets have been able to shift audiences towards digital subscription. The media system properties of these countries help to sustain features such as public service broadcasting and the local press through direct state funding. Strong regulatory involvement thus protects incumbents within the global media ecology. The institutional culture in which the news industries operate also contributes to this stability. A dispersed newspaper structure places journalism close to local communities, which engenders trust and loyalty. Ownership is often tied to identity, localism, and affinity, which encourages trust further. As the Scandinavian newspaper companies have consolidated, mergers and acquisitions have relied on institutional notions of 'fit'. Ownership concentration has thus been less fraught with tension in this period than in the past. The move to attain scale advantages in the news industries by mergers and acquisitions used to be perceived with suspicion and even fear in the mass media era. In the digital transition, these buyers are rather looked upon as saviours. Better to be rescued by like-minded companies who share a cultural affinity with the media welfare state than to face Google and Facebook alone. To that end, ownership and editorial culture also shape the operational space in which companies can manoeuvre as they try to counteract income losses in the industry.

The return to enduring institutional forms such as subscription payment and chain ownership is likely illustrative of the extent to which the mixed welfare state economies of these countries define the space in which economic action can be taken. If economic actions are interest-driven, as Swedberg (2006) asserts, how actors seek to realise their interests depends on the direction that social relations give them. As institutions are "dominant models for how interests can be realized" (ibid., p. 12), these models need to be perceived as legitimate to be stable. The stability of such legitimacy depends on shared beliefs, norms, and rules as frameworks that direct action. Because society consists of ongoing activities rather than models or rules, and institutions only exist in action, patterned behaviour constitutes power. Change, or resistance to change, is thus dependent on how institutions act out their interest. Change, moreover, constitutes a realignment of interests, norms, and power. To that end, how the news industries behave to realise their economic interest in the face of platform power depends on the network of social relations in which action is perceived. News organisations thus have to manoeuvre in an extended network of interest. Decision-makers must consider what models of behaviour are acceptable to a range of actors within this space – the state that supports journalism financially; owners that expect a return on investments; advertisers that expect proven and effective reach and exposure; and platforms that expect complementarity and data-readiness.

Chyi and Tenenboim (2019a; 2019b) have suggested that U.S. newspapers should focus on protecting the print product. Not only do the printed editions represent the primary income for most newspapers in the U.S.; audiences also value the print product over the online edition. An online strategy would only serve to deplete the value of the core product, they argue. The print edition certainly represents one of journalism's enduring features, one that is both valued and valuable, even if that value is appreciated by a steadily decreasing segment of the audience. However, as reasonable as this encouragement is, the difficulty with which economic interest can be realised with this model, given the migration of advertising towards the platform economy, demonstrates the extent to which newspapers must realign their interest towards the needs of new power holders in the media ecosystem.

The shift towards AI technology thus holds an entirely different set of properties for journalism than the shift to online publication. Journalism has undergone two phases of digitalisation, where the first was about adjusting to the needs of audiences in the online sphere (expecting content to be free), and the second is about adjusting to the needs of platforms in the algorithmic sphere (expecting content to be datafiable). As the playing field shifts, journalism's adherence to the enduring forms of organising news production is illustrative of the institutional power struggle at play. Returning to the basics, journalism is mobilising its institutional assets. In the face of platform economics, norms, rules, and values still play a role in directing interest-driven action. The value of the journalistic institution and its organisational forms may thus still hold power as a model for interest realisation – one based on principles of free expression, oversight, transparency, and professional curation – values that are direct opposites to the values of the platforms.

Key takeaways

The key takeaways from the analysis presented in this book can be summarised as follows:

- Journalism is still undergoing digital transformations. Local newspapers are particularly struggling as business models shift towards the AI-driven platform economy, in large part because they never fully completed the first digital transition to digital, online production.
- As much as communication welfare is supported by a diverse ownership structure, independent ownership is becoming less and less tenable in the platform economy. Scale advantages are necessary to enable platform alignment.
- Two-sided markets still guide business model thinking within the industry. As the balance of income shifts towards audience revenue, news organisations should consider how to capitalise on brand power to recapture their value as attractive spaces for advertising.
- Journalism may here find leverage in its enduring economic and organisational features as carriers of institutional strength. While long-term strategic thinking might be difficult in this fast-moving landscape, there is perhaps also a quality in the resistance to change observed in the news industries.
- Hence, while media management scholarship tends to focus on the urgency for managerial action (or reaction) to these developments, institutional inertia might also be a signal that not everything is broken in the news industries. Inertia might be a sign that some features are worthy of protection.

- And finally, while critical political economy scholarship tends to blame the profit motive for everything that is wrong with the media industries, profit seeking behaviour is also an expression of institutional interests acted out. How the markets for news are constituted thus reflects long-standing arrangements that are currently undergoing severe disruption, the reactions to which are institutional in nature.

How to approach the markets for news in the future

Scholarship sees the markets for news either as sites of struggle over power and welfare distribution, or as processes of bringing products to market. Research on the platform ecology, discussed in the previous chapter, demonstrates how digital content markets are both. Datafication logics are about complementarity, and platforms tend to scale towards lock-in. The technological and economic processes that bring products to market in the platform economy therefore contain a power struggle with welfare distribution properties. As revenue moves out of national markets towards the global level, welfare is redistributed away from established media systems. The space in which competitive advantage can be realised has therefore expanded, the resources that enable competitive advantage have migrated, and the information on which decisions can be made has become more obscure.

How we research the markets for news going forward therefore depends on how the business models of the news industries develop. As markets grow more intertwined, however, we also need to consider how revenue is generated by the network of actors in the extended platform ecology, and how it impacts journalism as a business. I suspect that we also need to reconsider how relevant and effective established economic principles and models applied to the media really are in explaining what is going on with the news industries. It is certainly time to re-evaluate core assumptions about the product market for journalism, competitive strategy, free-riding, and market failure, and how it applies to journalism in the networked platform economy. To do that, we need to understand how the digital infrastructure works as a market, as a system of distribution, and as a network of actors. Communication infrastructures are expanding to the point where platform technologies determine the space where communicative power is played out. As the markets for news grow more dependent on this infrastructure, we need to reassess what infrastructure power means for the principles of universal access, freedom of information, and freedom of expression, on which journalism relies.

There are many ways to approach this new reality for news media theoretically. The fact that much of the data needed to perform analyses at this level is difficult to attain suggests that research needs to be transparent, multi-disciplinary, and collaborative to grasp the many aspects that shape the markets for news in the platform economy. All the dimensions treated by the theories discussed in this book are present in the problems that characterise this space – power and welfare, governance and regulation, entrepreneurialism and innovation, and institutional norms and values. What this book has hopefully demonstrated is that economic realities are necessary to understand how media industries' owners and managers act and react in the face of disruption. Money is part of the institution of journalism because it motivates action. How revenue is attained impacts the organisation and performance of journalism. And how that revenue is realised depends on the institutional and media systems context in which news industries operate.

References

Aalberg, T., Van Aelst, P., & Curran, J. (2010). Media systems and the political information environment: A cross-national comparison. *The International Journal of Press/Politics*, *15*(3), 255–271.

Adorno, T. W., & Horkheimer, M. (1997). *Dialectic of enlightenment: Philosophical fragments*. Verso.

Albarran, A. B (2006). Historical trends and patterns in media management research. In A. B. Albarran, S. M. Chan-Olmsted, & M. O. Wirth (Eds.), *Handbook of media management and economics* (pp. 3–22). Lawrence Erlbaum Associates.

Albarran, A. B. (2010). *The media economy*. Routledge.

Albarran, A. B. (2017). *The media economy* (3rd ed.). Routledge.

Ali, C. (2016). The merits of merit goods: Local journalism and public policy in a time of austerity. *Journal of Information Policy*, *6*(1), 105–128.

Allern, S., & Blach-Ørsten, M. (2011). The news media as a political institution: A Scandinavian perspective. *Journalism Studies*, *12*(1), 92–105.

Allern, S., & Pollack, E. (2019). Journalism as a public good: A Scandinavian perspective. *Journalism*, *20*(11), 1423–1439.

Altmeppen, K-D., Hollifield, C. A., & van Loon, J. (2017). Value-oriented media management: What, why, and what for? An introduction to this volume. In K-D. Altmeppen, C. A. Hollifield, & van Loon, J. (Eds.), *Value-oriented media management: Decision making between profit and responsibility* (pp. 1–18). Springer.

Ambelu, A. A., Ali, A. C., & Skjerdal, T. S. (2021). An investigation on the perspectives of political economy: The case of ethiopian broadcasting corporation (EBC). *East African Journal of Social Sciences and Humanities*, *6*(2), 67–82.

Anderson, C. (01.10.2004). The long tail. *Wired*.

Anderson, C. (2006). *The long tail: Why the future of business is selling less of more*. Hachette UK.

Anderson, C. W., & De Maeyer, J. (2015). Objects of journalism and the news. *Journalism*, *16*(1), 3–9.

Anderson, C. W., Bell, E., & Shirky, C. (2015). Post-industrial journalism: Adapting to the present. *Geopolitics, History & International Relations*, *7*(2), 32–123.

Anderson, S. P., Foros, Ø., & Kind, H. J. (2010). Hotelling competition with multi-purchasing: Time Magazine, Newsweek, or both? *Working paper, 21/10*. The Norwegian School of Economics.

Andrejevic, M. (2007). Surveillance in the digital enclosure. *The Communication Review*, *10*(4), 295–317.

Armstrong, M. (2006). Competition in two-sided markets. *The RAND Journal of Economics*, *37*(3), 668–691.

Badr, Z. (2021). More or more of the same: Ownership concentration and media diversity in Egypt. *The International Journal of Press/Politics*, *26*(4), 774–796.

Baines, D., & Kennedy, C. (2010). An education for independence: Should entrepreneurial skills be an essential part of the journalist's toolbox? *Journalism Practice*, *4*(1), 97–113.

Baker, C. E. (2006). *Media concentration and democracy: Why ownership matters*. Cambridge University Press.

Ballon, P., & Van Heesvelde, E. (2011). ICT platforms and regulatory concerns in Europe. *Telecommunications Policy*, *35*(8), 702–714.

Barland, J. (2013). Innovation of new revenue streams in digital media. *Nordicom Review*. *34*, 99–112.

Barney, J. (1991). Firm resources and sustained competitive advantage. *Journal of Management*, *17*(1), 99–120.

Baum, M. A., & Zhukov, Y. M. (2019). Media ownership and news coverage of international conflict. *Political Communication*, *36*(1), 36–63.

Baumann, S. (2020). Guest editor's introduction: Strategic media management at a junction. *Journal of Media Business Studies*, *17*(1), 1–12.

Beaulieu, A., & Leonelli, S. (2022). *Data and society: A critical introduction*. Sage.

Becker, L. B., Hollifield, C. A., Jacobsson, A., Jacobsson, E. M., & Vlad, T. (2009). Is more always better? Examining the adverse effects of competition on media performance. *Journalism Studies*, *10*(3), 368–385.

Belair-Gagnon, V., & Steinke, A. J. (2020). Capturing digital news innovation research in organizations, 1990–2018. *Journalism Studies*, *21*(12), 1724–1743.

Bell, E. (2016). Facebook is eating the world. *Columbia Journalism Review*, *7*(3).

Bell, E. J., Owen, T., Brown, P. D., Hauka, C., & Rashidian, N. (2017). *The platform press: How Silicon Valley reengineered journalism*. Tow Centre for Digital Journalism.

Benkler, Y. (2002). Freedom in the commons: Towards a political economy of information. *Duke Law Journal*, *52*, 1245–1276.

Benson, R. (2016). Institutional forms of media ownership and their modes of power. In M. Eide, H. Sjøvaag, & L. O. Larsen (Eds.), *Journalism reexamined: Digital challenges and professional reorientations. Lessons from northern Europe* (pp. 29–47). Intellect.

Benson, R. (2018). Can foundations solve the journalism crisis? *Journalism*, *19*(8), 1059–1077.

Benson, R., Neff, T., & Hessérus, M. (2018). Media ownership and public service news: How strong are institutional logics? *The International Journal of Press/Politics*, *23*(3), 275–298.

Berg, C. E., Lowe, G. F., & Lund, A. B. (2013). A market failure perspective on value creation in P. S. M. In, G. F. Lowe, & F. Martin (Eds.), *The value of public service media* (pp. 105–126). Nordicom.

Berry, S. T., & Waldfogel, J. (2001). Do mergers increase product variety? Evidence from radio broadcasting. *The Quarterly Journal of Economics, 116*(3), 1009–1025.

Berte, K., & De Bens, E. (2009). Newspapers go for advertising! Challenges and opportunities in a changing media environment. In B. Franklin (Ed.), *The future of newspapers* (pp. 63–74). Routledge.

Boczkowski, P. J. (2009). Materiality and mimicry in the journalism field. In B. Zelizer (Ed.), *The changing faces of journalism: Tabloidization, technology and truthiness* (pp. 66–77). Routledge.

Bode, L., & Vraga, E. K. (2018). Studying politics across media. *Political Communication, 35*(1), 1–7.

Bodó, B. (2019). Selling news to audiences: A qualitative inquiry into the emerging logics of algorithmic news personalization in European quality news media. *Digital Journalism, 7*(8), 1054–1075.

Brandstetter, B., & Schmalhofer, J. (2014). Paid content: A successful revenue model for publishing houses in Germany? *Journalism Practice, 8*(5), 499–507.

Braun, J. A. (2015). News programs: Designing MSNBC.com's online interfaces. *Journalism, 16*(1), 27–43.

Braun, J. A., & Eklund, J. L. (2019). Fake news, real money: Ad tech platforms, profit-driven hoaxes, and the business of journalism. *Digital Journalism, 7*(1), 1–21.

Bridges, J. A., Litman, B. R., & Bridges, L. W. (2002). Rosse's model revisited: Moving to concentric circles to explain newspaper competition. *The Journal of Media Economics, 15*(1), 3–19.

Briggs, M. (2012). *Entrepreneurial journalism: How to build what's next for news*. CQ Press.

Bruns, A. (2010). News produsage in a pro-am mediasphere: Why citizen journalism matters. In G. Meikle & G. Redden (Eds.), *News online: Transformations and continuities* (pp. 132–147). Palgrave.

Brüggemann, M., Engesser, S., Büchel, F., Humprecht, E., & Castro, L. (2014). Hallin and Mancini revisited: Four empirical types of western media systems. *Journal of Communication, 64*(6), 1037–1065.

Brüggemann, M., Humprecht, E., Kleis Nielsen, R., Karppinen, K., Cornia, A., & Esser, F. (2016). Framing the newspaper crisis: How debates on the state of the press are shaped in Finland, France, Germany, Italy, United Kingdom and United States. *Journalism Studies, 17*(5), 533–551.

Bucher, T. (2018). *If... then: Algorithmic power and politics*. Oxford University Press.

Capoano, E., & Ranieri, P. (2016). From laboratories to media labs: Proposal for actualization in journalism learning. *Journalism Research and Education Online, 1*(1), 40–56.

Carvajal, M., & García Avilés, J. A. (2008). From newspapers to multimedia groups: Business growth strategies of the regional press in Spain. *Journalism Practice, 2*(3), 453–462.

Casilli, A. A., & Posada, J. (2019). The platformization of labor and society. In M. Graham & W. H. Dutton (Eds.), *Society and the internet. How networks of information and communication and changing our lives* (pp. 293–306). Oxford University Press.

Cawley, A. (2019). Digital transitions: The evolving corporate frameworks of legacy newspaper publishers. *Journalism Studies*, *20*(7), 1028–1049.

Chadha, M. (2016). What I am versus what I do: Work and identity negotiation in hyperlocal news startups. *Journalism Practice*, *10*(6), 697–714.

Chaharbaghi, K.; Fendt, C., & Willis, R. (2003). Meaning, legitimacy and impact of business models on fast-moving environments. *Management Decision*, *41*(4), 372–382.

Chan-Olmsted, S. M. (2006). Issues in strategic management. In Albarran, A. B., Chan-Olmsted, S. M., & Wirth, M. O. (Eds.), *Handbook of Media Management and Economics* (pp. 161–180). Lawrence Erlbaum Associates.

Chan-Olmsted, S. M. (2019). A review of artificial intelligence adoptions in the media industry. *International Journal on Media Management*, *21*(3–4), 193–215.

Chatterjee, P., & Zhou, B. (2021). Sponsored content advertising in a two-sided market. *Management Science*, *67*(12), 7560–7574.

Choi, J. P., & Yang, S. (2021). Investigative journalism and media capture in the digital age. *Information Economics and Policy*, *57*, 100942.

Christensen, C. (1997). *The innovator's dilemma: When technologies cause great firms to fail*. Harvard Business Review Press.

Christensen, C. (2003). *The innovator's solution: Creating and sustaining successful growth*. Harvard Business Review Press.

Chyi, H. (2013). *Trial and error: US newspapers' digital struggles toward inferiority*. University of Navarra.

Chyi, H. I., & Tenenboim, O. (2019a). Charging more and wondering why readership declined? A longitudinal study of US newspapers' price hikes, 2008–2016. *Journalism Studies*, *20*(14), 2113–2129.

Chyi, H. I., & Tenenboim, O. (2019b). From analog dollars to digital dimes: A look into the performance of US newspapers. *Journalism Practice*, *13*(8), 988–992.

Colangelo, G. (2022). Enforcing copyright through antitrust? The strange case of news publishers against digital platforms. *Journal of Antitrust Enforcement*, *10*(1), 133–161.

Conboy, M., & Steel, J. (2009). The Future of Newspapers: Historical Perspective. In B. Franklin (Ed.), *The Future of Newspapers* (pp. 21–32). London.

Cook, C., & Sirkkunen, E. (2013). What's in a niche? Exploring the business model of online journalism. *Journal of Media Business Studies*, *10*(4), 63–82.

Corrigan, T. F. (2018). Making implicit methods explicit: Trade press analysis in the political economy of communication. *International Journal of Communication*, *12*, 2751–2772.

Coyle, Diane (2018). Platform dominance: The shortcomings of antitrust policy. In. M. Morre & D. Tambini (Eds.), *Digital dominance: The power of Google, Amazon, Facebook and Apple* (pp. 50–70). Oxford University Press.

Crawford, G. S. (2008). The discriminatory incentives to bundle in the cable television industry. *Quantitative Marketing and Economics*, *6*(1), 41–78.

Cunningham, S., & Flew, T. (2015). Reconsidering media economics: From orthodoxies to heterodoxies. *Media Industries*, *2*(1), 1–18.

Cunningham, S., Flew, T., & Swift, A. (2015). *Media economics*. Macmillan.

Curran, J., & Seaton, J. (2003). *Power without responsibility: The press, broadcasting, and new media in Britain* (6th ed.). Routledge.

Dahlberg, L. (2011). Web 2.0 divides: A critical political economy. *Media and Journalism 18* (10:1), 84–99.

Deuze, M. (2008). The changing context of news work: Liquid journalism for a monitorial citizenry. *International Journal of Communication*, *2*(18), 848–865.

Deuze, M., & Witschge, T. (2018). Beyond journalism: Theorizing the transformation of journalism. *Journalism*, *19*(2), 165–181.

DiMaggio, P. J., & Powell, W. W. (1991). The iron cage revisited: Institutional isomorphism and collective rationality in organizational fields. In P. J. DiMaggio & W. W. Powell (Eds.), *The new institutionalism in organizational analysis* (pp. 63–82). University of Chicago Press.

Dimmick, J. (2006). Media competition and levels of analysis. In A. B. Albarran, B. Mierzejewska, & J. Jung (Eds.), *Handbook of media management and economics* (pp. 350–367). Routledge.

Domingo, D. (2015). Research that empowers responsibility: Reconciling human agency with materiality. *Journalism*, *16*(1), 69–73.

Donders, K. (2019). Public service media beyond the digital hype: Distribution strategies in a platform era. *Media, Culture & Society*, *41*(7), 1011–1028

Doyle, G. (2013). *Understanding media economics* (2nd ed.). Sage.

Dwyer, P. (2015). Theorizing media production: The poverty of political economy. *Media, Culture & Society*, *37*(7), 988–1004.

Ekström, M., & Westlund, O. (2019). The dislocation of news journalism: A conceptual framework for the study of epistemologies of digital journalism. *Media and Communication*, *7*(1), 259–270.

Ekström, M., Johansson, B., & Larsson, L. (2006). Journalism and local politics: A study of scrutiny and accountability in Swedish journalism. *Journalism Studies*, *7*(2), 292–311.

Dörr, K. (2018). Ethical approaches to computational journalism. In S. A. Eldridge & B. Franklin (Eds.), *The routledge handbook of developments in digital journalism studies* (pp. 313–323). Routledge.

Edge, M. (2019). Are UK newspapers really dying? A financial analysis of newspaper publishing companies. *Journal of Media Business Studies*, *16*(1), 19–39.

Ekberg, S. (2020). Are opportunities and threats enough? A development of the labels of strategic issues. *Journal of Media Business Studies*, *17*(1), 13–32.

Ellis, G. (2011). *A Ghost in the chair: Trustee ownership and the sustenance of democratically significant journalism*. Dissertation. University of Auckland.

Engelstad, F., Larsen, H., & Rogstad, J. (2017). The public sphere in the Nordic model. In F. Elgelstad, H. Larsen, J. Rogstad, & K. Steen-Johnsen (Eds.), *Institutional change in the public sphere: Views on the Nordic model* (pp. 46–70). De Gruyter.

Entman, R. M. (1989). *Democracy without citizens: Media and the decay of American politics*. Oxford University Press.

Evans, D. S. (2003). Some empirical aspects of multi-sided platform industries. *Review of Network Economics*, *2*(3), 191–209.

Evens, T. (2018). Media economics and transformation in a digital Europe. In L. d'Haenens, H. Sousa, & J. Trappel (Eds.), *Comparative media policy, regulation and governance in Europe: Unpacking the policy cycle* (pp. 41–54). Intellect.

Feng, S., & Ots, M. (2018). Seeing native advertising production via the business model lens: The case of forbes's brandvoice unit. *Journal of Interactive Advertising*, *18*(2), 148–161.

Fengler, S., & Ruß-Mohl, S. (2008). Journalists and the information-attention markets: Towards an economic theory of journalism. *Journalism*, *9*(6), 667–690.

Fenton, N. (2007). Bridging the mythical divide: Political economy and cultural studies approaches to the analysis of the media. In E. Devereux (Ed.), *Media studies: Key issues and debates* (pp. 7–31). Sage.

Ferrer Conill, R. (2016). Camouflaging church as state: An exploratory study of journalism's native advertising. *Journalism Studies*, *17*(7), 904–914.

Ferrer-Conill, R., Karlsson, M., Haim, M., Kammer, A., Elgesem, D., & Sjøvaag, H. (2021). Toward 'cultures of engagement'? An exploratory comparison of engagement patterns on Facebook news posts. *New Media & Society*. https://doi.org/14614448211009246.

Ferrucci, P. (2020). It is in the numbers: How market orientation impacts journalists' use of news metrics. *Journalism*, *21*(2), 244–261.

Fjell, K., Foros, Ø., & Steen, F. (2010). *The economics of social networks: The winner takes it all?* Working Paper no. 42/10, The Norwegian School of Economics.

Flensburg, S., & Lai, S. S. (2020). Mapping digital communication systems: Infrastructures, markets, and policies as regulatory forces. *Media, Culture & Society*, *42*(5), 692–710.

Fletcher, R., & Nielsen, R. K. (2017). Are news audiences increasingly fragmented? A cross-national comparative analysis of cross-platform news audience fragmentation and duplication. *Journal of Communication*, *67*(4), 476–498.

Flew, T. (2012). Media as creative industries: Conglomeration and globalization as accumulation strategies in an age of digital media. In D. Winseck & D. Y. Jin (Eds.), *The political economies of media: The transformation of the global media industries* (pp. 84–100). Bloomsbury.

Fligstein, N. (1990). *The transformation of corporate control*. Harvard University Press.

Fligstein, N. (2001). Institutional entrepreneurs and cultural frames-The case of the European Union's Single Market Program. *European Societies*, *3*(3), 261–287.

Fligstein, N. (2015). What kind of re-imagining does economic sociology need? In P. Aspers & N. Dodd (Eds.), *Re-imagining economic sociology* (pp. 301–315). Oxford University Press.

Fligstein, N., & Calder, R. (2015). Architecture of markets. In R. A. Scott & S. M. Kosslyn (Eds.), *Emerging trends in the social and behavioral sciences* (pp. 1–14). Wiley.

Foster, R. (2012). *News plurality in a digital world*. Reuters Institute for the Study of Journalism.

Franklin, B. (Ed.) (2008). *Pulling Newspapers Apart: Analysing Print Journalism.* Routledge.

Gabszewicz, J. J., Laussel, D., & Sonnac, N. (2002). Press advertising and the political differentiation of newspapers. *Journal of Public Economic Theory*, *4*(3), 317–334.

Gabszewicz, J. J., Resende, J., & Sonnac, N. (2015). Media as multi-sided platforms. In R. G. Picard & S. S. Wildman (Eds.), *Handbook on the economics of the media* (pp. 3–35). Edward Elgar Publishing.

Gandy Jr, O. H. (1992). The political economy approach: A critical challenge. *Journal of Media Economics*, *5*(2), 23–42.

Garnham, N. (1995). Political economy and cultural studies: Reconciliation or divorce? *Critical Studies in Mass Communication*, *12*, 62–62.

Garnham, N. (1997). Amartya Sen's "capabilities" approach to the evaluation of welfare: Its application to communications. *Javnost-The Public*, *4*(4), 25–34.

Garnham, N. (2014). The political economy of communication revisited. In J. Wasko, G. Murdock, & H. Sousa (Eds.), *The handbook of political economy of communications* (pp. 41–61). John Wiley & Sons.

Garrahan, M. (2017, March 17) Advertisers sceptical on Google ad policy changes. *Financial Times*. https://www.ft.com/content/dea0e14e-0e59-11e7-a88c-50ba212dce4d

Gawer, A. (2014). Bridging differing perspectives on technological platforms: Toward an integrative framework. *Research Policy*, *43*(7), 1239–1249.

Giddens, A. (1984). *The constitution of society: Outline of the theory of structuration.* University of California Press.

Gillespie, T. (2010). The politics of 'platforms'. *New Media & Society*, *12*(3), 347–364.

Gillespie, T. (2014). The relevance of algorithms. *Media Technologies: Essays on Communication, Materiality, and Society*, *167*(2014), 167.

Gillespie, T. (2018). *Custodians of the internet: Platforms, content moderation, and the hidden decisions that shape social media.* Yale University Press.

Goyanes, M. (2014). An empirical study of factors that influence the willingness to pay for online news. *Journalism Practice*, *8*(6), 742–757.

Graham, P. (2006). Issues in political economy. In A. B. Albarran, S. M. Chan-Olmsted, & M. O. Wirth (Eds.), *Handbook of media management and economics* (pp. 493–519). Lawrence Erlbaum Associates.

Granovetter, M. (1985). Economic action and social structure: The problem of embeddedness. *American Journal of Sociology*, *91*(3), 481–510.

Graves, L., & Konieczna, M. (2015). Sharing the news: Journalistic collaboration as field repair. *International Journal of Communication*, *9*, 1–19.

Gynnild, A. (2014). Journalism innovation leads to innovation journalism: The impact of computational exploration on changing mindsets. *Journalism*, *15*(6), 713–730.

Hagiu, A. (2015). Strategic decisions for multisided platforms. *MIT Sloan Management Review*, *10*, 4–13.

Haim, M., Karlsson, M., Ferrer-Conill, R., Kammer, A., Elgesem, D., & Sjøvaag, H. (2021). You should read this study! It investigates scandinavian social media logics☝. *Digital Journalism*, *9*(4), 406–426.

Hallin, D. C., & Mancini, P. (2004). *Comparing media systems: Three models of media and politics*. Cambridge university press.

Hallin, D. C., & Papathanassopoulos, S. (2002). Political clientelism and the media: Southern Europe and Latin America in comparative perspective. *Media, Culture & Society 24*(2),175–195.

Hamilton, J. (2004). *All the news that's fit to sell: How the market transforms information into news*. Princeton University Press.

Hanitzsch, T., & Berganza, R. (2012). Explaining journalists' trust in public institutions across 20 countries: Media freedom, corruption, and ownership matter most. *Journal of Communication*, *62*(5), 794–814.

Hardy, J. (2014a). *Critical political economy of the media: An introduction*. Routledge.

Hardy, J. (2014b). Critical political economy of communications: A mid-term review. *International Journal of Media & Cultural Politics*, *10*(2), 189–202.

Hardy, J. (2017a). Money, (co) production and power: The contribution of critical political economy to digital journalism studies. *Digital Journalism*, *5*(1), 1–25.

Hardy, J. (2017b). Commentary: Branded content and media-marketing convergence. *The Political Economy of Communication*, *5*(1), 81–87.

Harms, B., Bijmolt, T. H., & Hoekstra, J. C. (2019). You don't fool me! Consumer perceptions of digital native advertising and banner advertising. *Journal of Media Business Studies*, *16*(4), 275–294.

Havens, T. (2014). Media industry sociology: Mainstream, critical, and cultural perspectives. In S. Waisbord (Ed.), *Media sociology: A reappraisal* (pp. 98–113). John Wiley & Sons.

Havens, T., Lotz, A. D., & Tinic, S. (2009). Critical media industry studies: A research approach. *Communication, Culture & Critique*, *2*(2), 234–253.

Helm, D. (2005). Consumers, citizens and members: Public service broadcasting and the BBC. In D. Helm (Ed.), *Can the market deliver? Funding public service television in the digital age* (pp. 1–21). Indiana University Press.

Helmond, A. (2015). The platformization of the web: Making web data platform ready. *Social Media+ Society*, *1*(2), 1–11.

Hendrickx, J. (2020). Trying to survive while eroding news diversity: Legacy news media's catch-22. *Journalism Studies*, *21*(5), 598–614.

Hendrickx, J., & Ranaivoson, H. (2021). Why and how higher media concentration equals lower news diversity: The Mediahuis case. *Journalism*, *22*(11), 2800–2815.

Hendrickx, J., Montero, E., Ranaivoson, H., & Ballon, P. (2021). Becoming the data-informed newsroom? The promotion of audience metrics in the newsroom and journalists' interactions with them. *Digital Journalism*, *9*(4), 427–442.

Herbert, D., Lotz, A. D., & Marshall, L. (2019). Approaching media industries comparatively: A case study of streaming. *International Journal of Cultural Studies*, *22*(3), 349–366.

Herbert, D., Lotz, A. D., & Punathambekar, A. (2020). *Media industry studies*. John Wiley & Sons.

Herman, E. S., & McChesney, R. W. (1997). *The global media: The new missionaries of corporate capitalism*. Bloomsbury Academic Press.

Hesmondhalgh, D. (2002). *The cultural industries*. Sage.

Hesmondhalgh, D. (2013). *The cultural industries* (3rd ed.). Sage.

Hess, K., & Waller, L (2017). Community and hyperlocal journalism: A 'sustainable' model? In B. Franklin & S. Eldridge II (Eds.), *The routledge companion to digital journalism studies* (pp. 194–203). Routledge.

Hindman, M. (2018). *The internet trap*. Princeton University Press.

Hintz, A., Dencik, L., & Wahl-Jorgensen, K. (2018). *Digital citizenship in a datafied society*. John Wiley & Sons.

Hjarvard, S., & Kammer, A. (2015). Online news: Between private enterprise and public subsidy. *Media, Culture & Society*, *37*(1), 115–123.

Hollifield, C. A. (2006). News media performance in hypercompetitive markets: An extended model of effects. *The International Journal on Media Management*, *8*(2), 60–69.

Holm, A. B., Günzel, F., & Ulhøi, J. P. (2013). Openness in innovation and business models: Lessons from the newspaper industry. *International Journal of Technology Management*, *61*(3/4), 324–348.

Holt, J., & Perren, A. (2019). Media industries: A decade in review. In M. Deuze (Ed.), *Making media: Production, practices, and professions* (pp. 31–44). Amsterdam University Press.

Horwitz, R. B. (2005). On media concentration and the diversity question. *The Information Society*, *21*(3), 181–204.

Høst, S. (2018). *Avisåret 2017*. [Newspapers in 2017] Report 86/2018. Høgskulen i Volda.

Hotelling, H. (1929). Stability in competition. *The Economic Journal*, *39*(153), 41–57.

Humprecht, E., & Esser, F. (2018). Diversity in online news: On the importance of ownership types and media system types. *Journalism Studies*, *19*(2), 1825–1847.

Ihlen, Ø., Skogerbø, E., & Allern, S. (2015). På jakt etter norsk politisk kommunikasjon: Kommentarartikkel. [Searching for a Norwegian political communication: Commentary] *Norsk medietidsskrift*, *22*(03), 1–13.

Jamil, S. (2021). Increasing accountability using data journalism: Challenges for the Pakistani journalists. *Journalism Practice*, *15*(1), 19–40.

Jarvis, J. (2009). *What would Google do?* Collins Business.

Jääsaari, J., & Olson, E. K. (2010). Journalistic norms, organizational identity and crisis decision-making in PSB news organization. In S. Norhstedt (Ed.), *Communicating risks: Towards the threat society* (pp. 73–96). Nordicom.

Jenkins, J., & Nielsen, R. K. (2018). *The digital transition of local news*. Reuters Institute for the Study of Journalism.

Jordan, T. (2020). *The digital economy*. Polity.

Kahneman, D. (2011). *Thinking, fast and slow*. Macmillan.

Kammer, A. (2016). A welfare perspective on Nordic media subsidies. *Journal of Media Business Studies*, *13*(3), 140–152.

Kammer, A., Boeck, M., Hansen, J. V., & Hauschildt, L. J. H. (2015). The free-to-fee transition: Audiences' attitudes toward paying for online news. *Journal of Media Business Studies*, *12*(2), 107–120.

Karimi, J., & Walter, Z. (2015). The role of dynamic capabilities in responding to digital disruption: A factor-based study of the newspaper industry. *Journal of Management Information Systems*, *32*(1), 39–81.

Kathuria, V., & Lai, J. C. (2020). The Case of Google 'Snippets': An IP Wrong that Competition Law Cannot Fix. Max Planck Institute for Innovation & Competition Research Paper, (20–13).

Kaye, J., & Quinn, S. (2010). *Funding journalism in the digital age: Business models, strategies, issues and trends*. Peter Lang.

Kellner, D. (2009). Media industries and media/cultural studies: An articulation. *Political Economy and Cultural Studies*, 1–47.

Kim, S. D. (2018). Political Economy of the Korean Media Industry. In D. Y. Jin & N. Kwak (Eds.), *Communication, digital media, and popular culture in Korea: Contemporary research and future prospects* (pp. 81–102). Lexington Books.

Kleis Nielsen, R., & Ganter, S. A. (2018). Dealing with digital intermediaries: A case study of the relations between publishers and platforms. *New Media & Society*, *20*(4), 1600–1617.

Klinger, U., & Svensson, J. (2015). The emergence of network media logic in political communication: A theoretical approach. *New Media & Society*, *17*(8), 1241–1257.

Kosterich, A. (2020). Managing news nerds: Strategizing about institutional change in the news industry. *Journal of Media Business Studies*, *17*(1), 51–68.

Kosterich, A., & Weber, M. S. (2018). Starting up the news: The impact of venture capital on the digital news media ecosystem. *International Journal on Media Management*, *20*(4), 239–262.

Kosterich, A., & Weber, M. S. (2019). Transformation of a modern newsroom workforce: A case study of NYC journalist network histories from 2011 to 2015. *Journalism Practice*, *13*(4), 431–457.

Krebs, I., Bachmann, P., Siegert, G., Schwab, R., & Willi, R. (2021). Non-journalistic competitors of news media brands on Google and YouTube: From solid competition to a liquid media market. *Journal of Media Business Studies*, *18*(1), 27–44.

Krumsvik, A. H. (2014). Mulige modeller for fordeling av nettinntekter. [Possible models for distribution of online revenue] *Norsk medietidsskrift*, *21*(02), 138–155.

Krumsvik, A. H., & Sundet, V. S. (2011). Etablerte medier og deres forutsetninger for fortjeneste: En komparativ analyse av konkurranseforholdene i norsk avis-, radio-og fjernsynsbransje. [Established media and their prerequisites for revenue: A comparative analysis of the competitive conditions in Norwegian newspaper, radio and television industries] *Norsk medietidsskrift*, *18*(3), 188–214.

Kunert, J., & Thurman, N. (2019). The form of content personalisation at mainstream, transatlantic news outlets: 2010–2016. *Journalism Practice*, *13*(7), 759–780.

Küng, L. (2007). Does media management matter? Establishing the scope, rationale, and future research agenda for the discipline. *Journal of Media Business Studies*, *4*(1), 21–39.

Küng, L. (2011). Managing strategy and maximizing innovation in media organizations. In M. Deuze (Ed.), *Managing media work* (pp. 43–56). Sage.

Küng, L. (2016). Why is media management research so difficult–and what can scholars do to overcome the field's intrinsic challenges? *Journal of Media Business Studies*, *13*(4), 276–282.

Küng, L. (2017). *Strategic management in the media: Theory to practice* (2nd ed.). Sage.

Lacy, S. (1988). The impact of intercity competition on daily newspaper content. *Journalism Quarterly*, *65*(2), 399–406.

Lacy, S. (1991). Effects of group ownership on daily newspaper content. *Journal of Media Economics*, *4*(1), 35–47.

Lacy, S. (2004). Fuzzy market structure and differentiation: One size does not fit all. In, R. G. Picard (Ed.), *Strategic responses to media market changes* (pp. 83–95). Jönköping University.

Lacy, S., & Noh, G. Y. (1997). Theory, economics, measurement, and the principle of relative constancy. *Journal of Media Economics*, *10*(3), 3–16.

Leckner, S., Tenor, C., & Nygren, G. (2019). What about the hyperlocals? The drivers, organization and economy of independent news media in Sweden. *Journalism Practice*, *13*(1), 68–89.

Lehtisaari, K., Villi, M., Grönlund, M., Lindén, C. G., Mierzejewska, B. I., Picard, R., & Roepnack, A. (2018). Comparing innovation and social media strategies in Scandinavian and US Newspapers. *Digital Journalism*, *6*(8), 1029–1040.

Lessig, L. (2002). *The future of ideas: The fate of the commons in a connected world*. Vintage.

Lewis, C. (2011). Non-Profit Journalism Entrepreneurialism in the United States. In D. A. Levy & R. G. Picard (Eds.), *Is there a better structure for news providers?* (pp. 97–111). Reuters Institute for the Study of Journalism.

Lindén, T. C. G. (2017). Algorithms for journalism: The future of news work. *The Journal of Media Innovations*, *4*(1), 60–76.

Litman, B. (1988). Microeconomic foundations. In R. E. Picard, J. P. Winter, M. E. McCombs & S. Lacy (Eds.), *Press concentration and monopoly: New perspectives on newspaper ownership and operation* (pp. 3–34). Ablex Publishing.

Lowrey, W. (2012). Journalism innovation and the ecology of news production: Institutional tendencies. *Journalism & Communication Monographs*, *14*(4), 214–287.

Lowrey, W., & Gade, P. J. (2011). Complexity, uncertainty, and journalistic change. In W. Lowrey & P. J. Gade (Eds.), *Changing the news: The forces shaping journalism in uncertain times* (pp. 3–21). Routledge.

Lund, A. B. (2007). Media markets in Scandinavia: Political economy aspects of convergence and divergence, *Nordicom Review*, *28*, 121–134.

Maijanen, P., von Rimscha, B., & Głowacki, M. (2019). Beyond the surface of media disruption: Digital technology boosting new business logics, professional practices and entrepreneurial identities. *Journal of Media Business Studies, 16*(3), 163–165.

Mansell, R. (2004). Political economy, power and new media. *New Media & Society, 6*(1), 96–105.

March, J. G., & Olsen, J. P. (1983). The new institutionalism: Organizational factors in political life. *American Political Science Review, 78*(3), 734–749.

Mathisen, B. R. (Ed.) (2010). *Lokaljournalistikk: Blind patriotisme eller kritisk korrektiv? [Local journalism: Blind patriotism or critical corrective?]* Høyskoleforlaget.

Mauri, A. J., & Michaels, M. P. (1998). Firm and industry effects within strategic management: An empirical examination. *Strategic Management Journal, 19*(3), 211–219.

McChesney, R. W. (1997). Standpoint: Wither communication? *Journal of Broadcasting and Electronic Media, 41*(4), 566–572.

McChesney, R. W. (2000). The political economy of communication and the future of the field. *Media, Culture & Society, 22*(1), 109–116.

McChesney, R. W. (2003). The problem of journalism: A political economic contribution to and explanation of the crisis in contemporary US journalism, *Journalism Studies, 4*(83), 299–329.

McChesney, R. W. (2013). *Digital disconnect: How capitalism is turning the Internet against democracy*. The New Press.

McCombs, M. E. (1988). Concentration, monopoly and content. In R. E. Picard, J. P. Winter, M. E. McCombs, & S. Lacy (Eds.), *Press concentration and monopoly: New perspectives on newspaper ownership and operation* (pp. 129–138) Ablex Publishing.

McDonald, P (Ed.) (2022). *The Routledge Companion to Media Industries*. Routledge.

McDowell, W. S. (2011). The brand management crisis facing the business of journalism. *The International Journal on Media Management, 13*(1), 37–51.

McIntyre, D. P., & Srinivasan, A. (2017). Networks, platforms, and strategy: Emerging views and next steps. *Strategic Management Journal, 38*(1), 141–160.

McManus, J. H. (1994). *Market-driven journalism: Let the citizen beware?* Sage.

Meehan, E. R. (1999). Commodity, culture, common sense: Media research and paradigm dialogue. *Journal of Media Economics, 12*(2), 149–163.

Meehan, E. R. (2002). Gendering the commodity audience: Critical media research, feminism, and political economy. In E. R. Meehan & E. Riordan (Eds.), *Sex and money: Feminism and political economy in the media* (pp. 209–222). University of Minnesota Press.

Meehan, E. R., & Torre, P. J. (2014). Markets in theory and markets in television. In J. Wasko, G. Murdock, & H. Sousa (Eds.), *The handbook of political economy of communications* (pp. 62–82). John Wiley & Sons.

Ménard, C., & Shirley, M. M. (Eds.) (2005). *Handbook of new institutional economics*. Springer.

Mensing, D. (2007). Online revenue business model has changed little since 1996. *Newspaper Research Journal*, *28*(2), 22–37.

Mensing, D., & Ryfe, D. (2013). Blueprint for change: From the teaching hospital to the entrepreneurial model of journalism education. *ISOJ The Official Research Journal of the International Symposium on Online Journalism*, *3*(2), 26–44.

Meyer, P. (2009). *The vanishing newspaper: Saving journalism in the information age*. University of Missouri Press.

Miège, B. (1989). *The capitalization of cultural production*. International General.

Mierzejewska, B. I. (2011). Media management in theory and practice. In M. Deuze (Ed.), *Managing media work* (pp. 13–30). Sage.

Mierzejewska, B., & Hollifield C. A. (2006). Theoretical approaches in media man-agement research. In A. Albarran, S. Chan-Olmsted, & M. O. Wirth (Eds.), *Handbook of media management and economics* (pp. 37–65). Erlbaum.

Miller, T. (2014). The political economy of media work and watching. In S. Waisbord (Ed.), *Media sociology: A reappraisal* (pp. 114–129). Polity.

Moran, R. E., & Usher, N. (2021). Objects of journalism, revised: Rethinking materiality in journalism studies through emotion, culture and 'unexpected objects'. *Journalism*, *22*(5), 1155–1172.

Mosco, V. (2008). Current trends in the political economy of communication. *Global Media Journal*, *1*, 45–63.

Mosco, V. (2009). *The political economy of communication* (2nd ed.). Sage.

Munger, K. (2020). All the news that's fit to click: The economics of clickbait media. *Political Communication*, *37*(3), 376–397.

Murdock, G. (1978). Blindspots about western Marxism: A reply to Dallas Smythe. *CTheory*, *2*(2), 109–115.

Murdock, G., & Golding, P. (2002). Digital possibilities, market realities: The contradictions of communications convergence. *Socialist Register*, *38*, 111–129.

Murdock, G., & Golding, P. (2005) Culture, communications and political economy. In J. Curran & M. Gurevitch (Eds.), *Mass media and society* (4th ed., pp. 60–83). Hodder.

Murdock, G., & Golding, P. (2016). Political economy and media production: A reply to Dwyer. *Media, Culture & Society*, *38*(5), 763–769.

Murschetz, P. C. (2020). State aid for independent news journalism in the public interest? A critical debate of government funding models and principles, the market failure paradigm, and policy efficacy. *Digital Journalism*, *8*(6), 720–739.

Napoli, P. M. (2020). Connecting journalism and public policy: New concerns and continuing challenges. *Digital Journalism*, *8*(6), 691–703.

Nechushtai, E. (2018). Could digital platforms capture the media through infrastructure? *Journalism*, *19*(8), 1043–1058.

Nee, R. C. (2013). Creative destruction: An exploratory study of how digitally native news nonprofits are innovating online journalism practices. *International Journal on Media Management*, *15*(1), 3–22.

Neff, G. (2015). Learning from documents: Applying new theories of materiality to journalism. *Journalism*, *16*(1), 74–78.

Nelson, J. L. (2018). And Deliver Us to Segmentation: The growing appeal of the niche news audience. *Journalism Practice*, *12*(2), 204–219.

Newman, N. (2012). *Reuters Institute digital news report 2012*. Reuters Institute for the Study of Journalism.

Newman, N., & Levy, D. A. L. (2013). *Reuters Institute digital news report 2013: Tracking the future of news*. Reuters Institute for the Study of Journalism.

Newman, N., & Levy, D. A. L. (2014). *Reuters Institute digital news report 2014: Tracking the future of news*. Reuters Institute for the Study of Journalism.

Newman, N., Levy, D. A. L., & Nielsen, R. K. (2015). *Reuters Institute digital news report 2015: Tracking the future of news*. Reuters Institute for the Study of Journalism.

Newman, N., Fletcher, R., Levy, D. A. L., & Nielsen, R. K. (2016). *Reuters Institute digital news report 2016*. Reuters Institute for the Study of Journalism.

Newman, N., Fletcher, R., Kalogeropoulos, A., Levy, D. A., & Nielsen, R. K. (2017). *Reuters institute digital news report 2017*. Reuters Institute for the Study of Journalism.

Newman, N., Fletcher, R., Kalogeropoulos, A., Levy, D. A., & Nielsen, R. K. (2018). *Reuters institute digital news report 2018*. Reuters Institute for the Study of Journalism.

Newman, N., Fletcher, R., Kalogeropoulos, A., Levy, D. A., & Nielsen, R. K. (2019). *Reuters institute digital news report 2019*. Reuters Institute for the Study of Journalism.

Newman, N., Fletcher, R., Schulz, A., Andi, S., & Nielsen, R. K. (2020). *Reuters institute digital news report 2020*. Reuters Institute for the Study of Journalism.

Newman, N., Fletcher, R., Schulz, A., Andi, S., Robertson, C. T., & Nielsen, R. K. (2021). *Reuters institute digital news report 2021* (10th ed.). Reuters Institute for the Study of Journalism.

Nicas, J. (2017, March 24) Google's YouTube has continued showing brands' ads with racist and other objectionable videos. *The Wall Street Journal*. https://www.wsj.com/articles/googles-youtube-has-continued-showing-brands-ads-with-racist-and-other-objectionable-videos-1490380551

Nieborg, D. B., & Poell, T. (2018). The platformization of cultural production: Theorizing the contingent cultural commodity. *New Media & Society*, *20*(11), 4275–4292.

Nielsen, R. K. (2016). The many crises of Western journalism: A comparative analysis of economic crises, professional crises, and crises of confidence. In J. C. Alexander, E. B. Breese, & M. Luengo (Eds.), *The crisis of journalism reconsidered* (pp. 77–97). Cambridge University Press.

Noam, E. M. (2009). *Media ownership and concentration in America*. Oxford University Press.

Noam, E. (2018). *Media and digital management*. Palgrave McMillan.

North, D. C. (1990). *Institutions, institutional change and economic performance*. Cambridge University Press.

NOU (2017:7). *Det norske mediemangfoldet: En styrket mediepolitikk for borgerne [Media diversity in Norway: A strengthened media policy for citizens]*. The Ministry of Culture.

Nygren, G., Leckner, S., & Tenor, C. (2018). Hyperlocals and legacy media: Media ecologies in transition. *Nordicom Review*, *39*(1), 33–49.

O'Brien, D., & Wellbrock, C. M. (2021). How the trick is done: Conditions of success in entrepreneurial digital journalism. *Digital Journalism*. https://doi.org/10.1080/21670811.2021.1287947.

Ohlsson, J. (2012). *The practice of newspaper ownership: Fifty years of control and influence in the Swedish local press*. The University of Stockholm.

Ohlsson, J., & Facht, U. (2017). *Ad wars: Digital challenges for ad-financed news media in the Nordic Countries*. Nordicom.

Ohlsson, J., & Sjøvaag, H. (2019). Protectionism vs. Non-interventionism: Two approaches to media diversity in commercial terrestrial television regulation. *Javnost: The Public*, *26*(1), 70–88.

Olsen, K. S. (2018). What we talk about when we talk about local journalism: Tacit knowledge during the digital shift. *Sur le Journalism*, *7*(2), 126–141.

Olsen, R. K., Pickard, V., & Westlund, O. (2020). Communal news work: COVID-19 calls for collective funding of journalism. *Digital Journalism*, *8*(5), 673–680.

Olsen, R. K., Kalsnes, B., & Barland, J. (2021). Do small streams make a big river? Detailing the diversification of revenue streams in newspapers' transition to digital journalism businesses. *Digital Journalism*. https://doi.org/10.1080/21670811.2021.1973905.

Olsson, E. K. (2009). Rule regimes in news organization decision making: Explaining diversity in the actions of news organizations during extraordinary events. *Journalism*, *10*(6), 758–776.

Ottosen, R., & Krumsvik, A. H. (2012). Digital challenges on the Norwegian media scene. *Nordicom Review*, *33*(2), 43–55.

Pantic, M. (2021). Local media in a digital market: Establishing niche and promoting original reporting to ensure sustainability. *Journalism Practice*. https://doi.org/10.1080/17512786.2021.1874483.

Park, D. J. (2017). Individualization, information asymmetry, and exploitation in the advertiser-driven digital era. *The Political Economy of Communication*, *5*(2), 22–44.

Parker, G. G., Van Alstyne, M. W., & Choudary, S. P. (2016). *Platform revolution: How networked markets are transforming the economy and how to make them work for you*. WW Norton & Company.

Parsons, P., Finnegan, J. J., & Benham, W. (1988). Editors and their roles. In R. E. Picard, J. P. Winter, M. E. McCombs, & S. Lacy (Eds.), *Press concentration and monopoly: New perspectives on newspaper ownership and operation* (pp. 91–104), Ablex Publishing.

Pavlik, J. V. (2013). A vision for transformative leadership: Rethinking journalism and mass communication education for the twenty-first century. *Journalism & Mass Communication Educator*, *68*(3), 211–221.

Pereira, C. (2009). Inequalities on the web: Strengths and weaknesses of a political economy analysis. *Media, Culture & Society*, *31*(2), 325–330.

Peterson, R. A., & Anand, N. (2004). The production of culture perspective. *Annual Review of Sociology*, *30*, 311–334.

Peterson-Salahuddin, C., & Diakopoulos, N. (2020). Negotiated autonomy: The role of social media algorithms in editorial decision making. *Media and Communication*, *8*(3), 27–38.

Picard, R. G. (1989). *Media economics: Concepts and issues*. Sage.

Picard, R. G. (2002). *The economics and financing of media companies*. Fordham University Press.

Picard, R. G. (2006). Historical trends and patterns in media economics. In A. B. Albarran, S. M. Chan-Olmsted, & M. O. Wirth (Eds.), *Handbook of Media Management and Economics* (pp. 23–36). Lawrence Erlbaum Associates.

Picard, R. G. (2008). Shifts in newspaper advertising expenditures and their implications for the future of newspapers. *Journalism Studies*, *9*(5), 704–716.

Picard, R. G. (2009a). Introduction: Changing structures and organization of newsrooms. *Journal of Media Business Studies*, *6*(1), 1–5.

Picard, R. G. (2009b). *Tremors, structural damage and some casualties, but no cataclysm: The news about news provision*. The U.S. Federal Trade Commission.

Picard, R. G. (2011). *The economics and financing of media companies*. Fordham University Press.

Picard, R. G. (2017). Funding digital journalism: The challenges of consumers and the economic value of news. In B. Franklin & S. Eldridge II (Eds.), *The Routledge Companion to Digital Journalism Studies* (pp. 147–154). Routledge.

Picard, R. G. (2018). The economics of journalism and news provision. In T. Vos (Ed.), *Journalism* (pp. 281–296). De Gruyter.

Picard, R. G., & Dal Zotto, C. (2016). The dimension of ownership and control of media. In P. Valcke, M. Sükösd, & R. G. Picard (Eds.), *Media pluralism and diversity: Concepts, risks and global trends* (pp. 54–66). Palgrave.

Picard, R. G., & Lowe, G. F. (2016). Questioning media management scholarship: Four parables about how to better develop the field. *Journal of Media Business Studies*, *13*(2), 61–72.

Picard, R. G., & Van Weezel, A. (2008). Capital and control: Consequences of different forms of newspaper ownership. *The International Journal on Media Management*, *10*(1), 22–31.

Pickard, V. (2013). Social democracy or corporate libertarianism? Conflicting media policy narratives in the wake of market failure. *Communication Theory*, *23*(4), 336–355.

Pickard, V. (2014). The great evasion: Confronting market failure in American media policy. *Critical Studies in Media Communication*, *31*(2), 153–159.

Pickard, V. (2015). *America's battle for media democracy: The triumph of corporate libertarianism and the future of media reform*. Cambridge University Press.

Pickard, V. (2017). Rediscovering the news: Journalism studies' three blind spots. In P. J. Boczkowski & C. W. Anderson (Eds.), *Remaking the news: Essays on the future of journalism scholarship in the digital age* (pp. 47–60). MIT Press.

Pickard, V. (2019). The violence of the market. *Journalism*, *20*(1), 154–158.

Peters, C. (2019). Journalism needs a better argument: Aligning public goals with the realities of the digital news and information landscape. *Journalism*, *20*(1), 73–76.

Perloff, J. M., & Salop, S. C. (1985). Equilibrium with product differentiation. *The Review of Economic Studies*, *52*(1), 107–120.

Plantin, J. C., Lagoze, C., Edwards, P. N., & Sandvig, C. (2018). Infrastructure studies meet platform studies in the age of Google and Facebook. *New Media & Society*, *20*(1), 293–310.

Porter, M. E. (1980). *Competitive strategy: Techniques for analyzing industries and competitors*. Free Press.

Porter, M. E. (1985). *Competitive advantage: Creating and sustaining superior performance*. Free Press.

Postigo, H. (2016). The socio-technical architecture of digital labor: Converting play into YouTube money. *New Media & Society*, *18*(2), 332–349.

Reporters Without Borders (2021). *2021 World press freedom index*. https://rsf.org/en/ranking/2021

Rieder, B., & Sire, G. (2014). Conflicts of interest and incentives to bias: A microeconomic critique of Google's tangled position on the Web. *New Media & Society*, *16*(2), 195–211.

Rochet, J. C., & Tirole, J. (2006). Two-sided markets: A progress report. *The RAND Journal of Economics*, *37*(3), 645–667.

Rohn U., & Evens, T. (Eds.) (2020). *Media management matters: Challenges and opportunities for bridging theory and practice*. Routledge.

Rosse, J. N. (1975). Economic limits of press responsibility. *Studies in Industry Economics*, *56*, 12–18.

Ruotolo, C. (1988). Monopoly and socialization. In R. E. Picard, J. P. Winter, M. E. McCombs, & S. Lacy (Eds.), *Press concentration and monopoly: New perspectives on newspaper ownership and operation* (pp. 117–125). Ablex Publishing Corporation.

Ruotsalainen, J., & Heinonen, S. (2015). Media ecology and the future ecosystemic society. *European Journal of Futures Research*, *3*(1), 1–10.

Russell, F. M. (2019). The new gatekeepers: An Institutional-level view of Silicon Valley and the disruption of journalism. *Journalism Studies*, *20*(5), 631–648.

Ryfe, D. (2021). The economics of news and the practice of news production. *Journalism Studies*, *22*(1), 60–76.

Scalzini, S. (2021). The new related right for press publishers: What way forward?. In E. Rosati (Ed.), *The Routledge Handbook of EU Copyright Law* (pp. 101–119). Routledge.

Schiller,H. (1969). *Mass communications and American Empire*. Beacon.

Schlosberg, J. (2016). *Media ownership and agenda control: The hidden limits of the information age*. Taylor & Francis.

Schultz, I. (2007). Fra partipresse over omnibuspresse til segmentpresse. [From party press via omnibus press to segmented press]. *Journalistica*, *2*(5), 5–26.

Sen, A. (1986). Social choice theory. *Handbook of Mathematical Economics*, *3*, 1073–1181.

Siapera, E. (2013). Platform infomediation and journalism. *Culture Machine*, *14*, 1–28.

Siles, I., & Boczkowski, P. J. (2012). Making sense of the newspaper crisis: A critical assessment of existing research and an agenda for future work. *New Media & Society*, *14*(8), 1375–1394.

Singer, J. B. (2004). Strange bedfellows? The diffusion of convergence in four news organizations. *Journalism Studies*, *5*(1), 3–18.

Singer, J. B. (2010). Quality control: Perceived effects of user-generated content on newsroom norms, values and routines. *Journalism Practice*, *4*(2), 127–142.

Sjøvaag, H. (2014a). Homogenisation or differentiation? The effects of consolidation in the regional newspaper market. *Journalism Studies*, *15*(5), 511–521.

Sjøvaag, H. (2014b). The principles of regulation and the assumption of media effects. *Journal of Media Business Studies*, *11*(1), 5–20.

Sjøvaag, H. (2019). *Journalism between the state and the market*. Routledge.

Sjøvaag, H., & Ohlsson, J. (2019). Media ownership and journalism. In H. Örnebring (Ed.), *Oxford encyclopedia of journalism studies*. Oxford University Press

Sjøvaag, H., & Owren, T. (2021a). The non-substitutability of local news? Advertising and the decline of journalism's umbrella market model. *Nordicom Review*, *42*(1), 1–15.

Sjøvaag, H., & Owren, T. (2021b). Risk perception in newspaper chains: Threats, uncertainties and corporate boundary work. *Journalism*. https://doi.org/10.1177/14648849211031363.

Sjøvaag, H., & Pedersen, T. A. (2019). Female voices in the news: Structural conditions of gender representations in Norwegian newspapers. *Journalism & Mass Communication Quarterly*, *96*(1), 215–238.

Sjøvaag, H., Pedersen, T. A., & Laegreid, O. M. (2019). Journalism and the political structure. *Nordicom Review*, *40*(2), 63–89.

Sjøvaag, H., Pedersen, T. A., & Owren, T. (2019). Is public service broadcasting a threat to commercial media? *Media, Culture & Society*, *41*(6), 808–827.

Sjøvaag, H., Owren, T., & Borgen, T. (2021). Strategic and organisational fit in corporate news markets: A principal-agent approach to studying newspaper mergers. *Journalism Practice*, *15*(8), 1181–1198.

Sjøvaag, H., Stavelin, E., Karlsson, M., & Kammer, A. (2019). The hyperlinked Scandinavian news ecology: The unequal terms forged by the structural properties of digitalisation. *Digital Journalism*, *7*(4), 507–531.

SKLS (2018). *Nye medier, nye vaner, nye tider [New media, new habits, new times]*. The Ministry of Culture.

Slaatta, T. (2015). Print versus digital in Norwegian newspapers. *Media, Culture & Society*, *37*(1), 124–133.

Slot, M. (2021). About introvert incumbents and extravert start-ups: An exploration of the dialectics of collaborative innovation in the Dutch journalism field. *Journalism*, *22*(2), 414–429.

Slauter, W. (2019). *Who owns the news? A history of copyright*. Stanford University Press.

SOU (2016:80). *En gränsöverskridande mediepolitik: För upplysning, engagemang och ansvar [A boundary breaking media policy; For information, engagement and responsibility]*. The Ministry of Culture.

Smith, A. (2010[1776]). *The Wealth of Nations: An inquiry into the nature and causes of the Wealth of Nations*. Harriman House Limited.

Smythe, D. W. (1977). Communications: Blindspot of western Marxism. *CTheory*, *1*(3), 1–27.

Soloski, J. (1979). Economics and management: The real influence of newspaper groups. *Newspaper Research Journal*, *1*(1), 19–29.

Soloski, J. (1989). News reporting and professionalism: Some constraints on the reporting of the news. *Media, Culture & Society*, *11*(2), 207–228.

Stahl, F., & Maass, W. (2004). Strategies for selling paid content on newspaper and magazine web sites: An empirical analysis of bundling and splitting of news and magazine articles. *International Journal on Media Management*, *6*(1–2), 59–66.

Steensen, S., & Ahva, L. (2015). Theories of journalism in a digital age: An exploration and introduction. *Digital Journalism*, *3*(1), 1–18.

Steensen, S., Larsen, A. M. G., Hågvar, Y. B., & Fonn, B. K. (2019). What does digital journalism studies look like? *Digital Journalism*, *7*(3), 320–342.

Swedberg, R. (2006). *The toolkit of economic sociology*. SOCIUS Working Papers No. 4/2006.

Swedberg, R., Himmelstrand, U., & Brulin, G. (1987). The paradigm of economic sociology. *Theory and Society*, *16*(2), 169–213.

Syvertsen, T., Mjøs, O. J., Moe, H., & Enli, G. S. (2014). *The media welfare state: Nordic media in the digital era*. University of Michigan Press.

Tameling, K., & Broersma, M. (2013). De-converging the newsroom: Strategies for newsroom change and their influence on journalism practice. *International Communication Gazette*, *75*(1), 19–34.

Thomas, R. J. (2016). In defense of journalistic paternalism. *Journal of Media Ethics*, *31*(2), 86–99.

UN Democracy Index (2020). https://www.fn.no/Statistikk/demokratiindeksen

Usher, N. (2021). *News for the rich, white, and blue: How place and power distort American Journalism*. Columbia University Press.

Van Alstyne, M. W., Parker, G. G., & Choudary, S. P. (2016). Pipelines, platforms, and the new rules of strategy. *Harvard Business Review*, *94*(4), 54–62.

Van der Wurff, R. (2005). Online competition and performance of news and information markets in the Netherlands, *Gazette*, *67*(1), 9–26.

Van der Wurff, R. (2011). Are news media substitutes? Gratifications, contents, and uses, *Journal of Media Economics*, *24*(3), 139–157.

Van Dijck, J., & Poell, T. (2013). Understanding social media logic. *Media and Communication*, *1*(1), 2–14.

Van Dijck, J., Poell, T., & De Waal, M. (2018). *The platform society: Public values in a connective world*. Oxford University Press.

Van Kranenburg, H., & Hogenbrink, A. (2006). Issues in market structure. In A. B. Albarran, S. M. Chan-Olmsted, & M. O. Wirth (Eds.,) *Handbook of media management and economics* (pp. 325–344). Lawrence Erlbaum Associates.

Varadarajan, R., & Yadav, M. S. (2009). Marketing strategy in an internet-enabled environment: A retrospective on the first ten years of JIM and a prospective on the next ten years. *Journal of Interactive Marketing*, *23*(1), 11–22.

Varadarajan, R., Yadav, M. S., & Shankar, V. (2008). First-mover advantage in an Internet-enabled market environment: Conceptual framework and propositions. *Journal of the Academy of Marketing Science*, *36*(3), 293–308.

Vining, A. R., & Weimer, D. L. (1992). Welfare economics as the foundation for public policy analysis: Incomplete and flawed but nevertheless desirable. *The Journal of Socio-Economics*, *21*(1), 25–37.

Von Rimscha, B. (2016). Business models of media industries; Describing and promoting commodification. In G. F. Lowe & C. Brown (Eds.), *Managing media firms and industries: What's so special about media management?* (pp. 207–222). Springer.

Wadbring, I. (2007). The role of free dailies in a segregated society. *Nordicom Review*, *28*, 135–147.

Walck, P. E., Cruikshank, S. A., & Kalyango Jr, Y. (2015). Mobile learning: Rethinking the future of journalism practice and pedagogy. *Journalism & Mass Communication Educator*, *70*(3), 235–250.

Walters, P. (2020). A public good: Can government really save the press? *Journalism*. https://doi.org/10.1077/1464884920982404.

WAN-IFRA (2006). *Business models of newspaper publishing companies: Where news?* The Media Future Research Initiative, Report no. 1, www.ifra.com/wherenrews.

Wang, Q. (2018). Dimensional field theory: The adoption of audience metrics in the journalistic field and cross-field influences. *Digital Journalism*, *6*(4), 472–491.

Wasko, J. (2005). Studying the political economy of media and information. *Comunicação e Sociedade*, *7*, 25–48.

Wasko, J. (2014). The study of the political economy of the media in the twenty-first century. *International Journal of Media & Cultural Politics*, *10*(3), 259–271.

Wasko, J. (2018). Studying political economies of communication in the twenty-first century. *Javnost: The Public*, *25*(1–2), 233–239.

Welbers, K., & Opgenhaffen, M. (2019). Presenting news on social media: Media logic in the communication style of newspapers on Facebook. *Digital Journalism*, *7*(1), 45–62.

Wildman, S. S. (2006). Paradigms and analytical frameworks in modern economics and media economics. In A. B. Albarran, S. M. Chan-Olmsted, & M. O. Wirth (Eds.), *Handbook of media management and economics* (pp. 67–90). Lawrence Erlbaum Associates.

Will, A., & Gossel, B. (2017). Media markets, value and the unique: Consequences and implications for media management from Karpik's new economics sociology perspective. In K-D. Altmeppen, C. A. Hollifield, & van Loon, J. (Eds.), *Value-oriented media management: Decision making between profit and responsibility* (pp. 65–81). Springer.

Williams, R. (1983). *Culture and society, 1780–1950*. Columbia University Press.

Winseck, D. (Ed.). (2011). *The political economies of media: The transformation of the global media industries*. Bloomsbury Publishing.

Winseck, D. (2012). The political economies of media and the transformation of the global media industries. In D. Winseck (Ed.), *The political economies of media: The transformation of the global media industries* (pp. 3–48). Bloomsbury Publishing.

Winseck, D. (2017). The geopolitical economy of the global internet infrastructure. *Journal of Information Policy*, *7*(1), 228–267.

Winseck, D. (2019). Media concentration in the age of the internet and mobile phones. In M. Deuze & M. Prenger (Eds.), *Making media: Production, practices, and professions* (pp. 175–190). Amsterdam University Press.

Wirtz, B., & Elsäßer, M. (2017). Business models in media markets. In K-D. Altmeppen, C. A. Hollifield, & van Loon, J. (Eds.), *Value-oriented media management: Decision making between profit and responsibility* (pp. 33–48). Springer.

Zerbe Jr, R. O., & McCurdy, H. E. (1999). The failure of market failure. *Journal of Policy Analysis and Management*, *18*(4), 558–578.

Zott, C., Amit, R., & Massa, L. (2011). The business model: Recent developments and future research. *Journal of Management*, *37*(4), 1019–1042.

Index

For Product Safety Concerns and Information please contact our EU representative GPSR@taylorandfrancis.com
Taylor & Francis Verlag GmbH, Kaufingerstraße 24, 80331 München, Germany

www.ingramcontent.com/pod-product-compliance
Lightning Source LLC
LaVergne TN
LVHW020641100826
845148LV00012B/2288

* 9 7 8 0 3 6 7 5 3 3 9 6 0 *